Spirit and Life

The Holy Sacraments of the Catholic Church

Created by
Rose Rea

Designed by Gemma Hawes
Photography by Peter Weldon

SOPHIA INSTITUTE PRESS
Manchester, New Hampshire

Sophia Institute Press
Box 5284, Manchester, NH 03108
1-800-888-9344
www.SophiaInstitute.com

Sophia Institute Press® is a registered trademark of Sophia Institute.

Library of Congress Cataloging-in-Publication Data

Names: Rea, Rose, author.
Title: Spirit and life : the holy sacraments of the Catholic Church / created by Rose Rea ; designed by Gemma Hawes ; photography by Peter Weldon.
Description: Manchester, New Hampshire : Sophia Institute Press, 2019. | Includes bibliographical references and index.
Identifiers: LCCN 2018059774 | ISBN 9781622828128 (hardcover : alk. paper)
Subjects: LCSH: Sacraments—Catholic Church.
Classification: LCC BX2200 .R37 2019 | DDC 234/.16088282—dc23 LC record available at https://lccn.loc.gov/2018059774

First printing

Table of Contents

THE SACRAMENTS OF HEALING

THE SACRAMENTS AT THE SERVICE OF COMMUNION

Foreword

I'll always remember the first time I saw the waves rolling onto the shore of the Sea of Galilee. I was struck by their sheer beauty and the fact that so much of Jesus' ministry occurred around and on the sea. He fished and taught while on the sea. He calmed the waters, and walked on them. In my imagination as I gazed at the sea, I could see Jesus calling the apostles to follow him, preaching from a boat, or preparing a meal for them after His Resurrection.

As the pinnacle of God's creation, we human beings, in whom body and soul are woven together, have a desire embedded in us a desire to experience the world God has created. But in the words of St. Paul, we "see in a mirror dimly" while we are on this side of heaven (1 Cor. 13:12). For the most part, the spiritual world is not readily accessible to our physical senses, except, most notably, in the seven sacraments.

In the sacraments, we tangibly experience the grace and power of God. We receive God's grace—His very life—when we feel the holy water poured over our heads in Baptism, when we hear the words of absolution in Reconciliation, when we smell the sacred chrism used in Confirmation, and when we consume the Body and Blood of Christ in the Eucharist. The sacraments are both a window into heaven and a channel of grace for us during our life on earth.

Nellie Organ, an Irish girl who lived for a brief four and a half years in the early 1900s, experienced this reality in a truly wonderful way. Although she suffered from scoliosis and tuberculosis and rarely left her bed, this little girl developed a deep devotion to Jesus in the Blessed Sacrament, whom she called the "Hidden Jesus." The first time she saw Jesus exposed in a monstrance, she exclaimed, "There He is, there is Holy God!"

She longed to receive Jesus in the Eucharist, to "have Holy God in my heart," even though at that time, the age for receiving First Communion was twelve. Through the intercession of the sisters who cared for her, the local bishop gave permission for her to receive her First Communion. A priest who was present for that occasion described Nellie's thanksgiving after her First Communion: "She seemed in an ecstasy, and all remarked on the heavenly light that illuminated the child's countenance."

When Pope Pius X was told the story of Nellie and her longing for the Eucharist, he replied, "There! That is the sign for which I was waiting." A few months later he issued *Quam Singulari*, which lowered the age of Communion for children to around age seven, where it remains today.

Through her childlike faith, little Nellie was able to encounter the grace and love of the Holy Trinity in ways that revealed the spiritual reality that lies beneath the outward signs of the sacraments.

In my ministry as a bishop, I have witnessed in young children and in the sick the deep faith that they radiate as they receive the sacraments. I spoke with a young boy of four who had brain cancer and whose only desire was to receive Communion prior to his surgery so that he could have Jesus with him. He understood so well the love of the Holy Spirit and Jesus for him, that I confirmed him and gave him First Eucharist. Today he is healthy and continues in his faith journey. It is always a joy to see his reverence, receptivity, and love in receiving Holy Communion.

Spirit and Life: The Holy Sacraments of the Catholic Church invites you into this privileged space of encounter with the living God, with the God who became flesh for our sake and continues to live among us in the sacraments. I pray that as you read this book, you will be led to a deeper intimacy with the Father, the Son, and the Holy Spirit and, through that experience of love, grow in love for God and neighbor.

—**Archbishop Samuel J. Aquila**

Preface

"Your words are spirit and life, O Lord, life everlasting."

This beautiful hymn sums up what Christ says in John 6:63, "It is the spirit that gives life, while the flesh is of no avail. The words I have spoken to you are spirit and life." In the writings of the Fathers of the Church, the word "sacrament" was used to signify something sacred or mysterious, a concrete reality of an invisible grace. These seven sacred gifts, instituted by Christ Himself, cleanse and strengthen us along our earthly journey, assisting us with divine grace as we strive for our final goal, heaven.

Explore the sacraments from a new perspective as you wander through the pages of this book. Each chapter begins with Sacred Scripture and an excerpt from the *Catechism of the Catholic Church* on one of the sacraments. Then follows a commentary on the sacrament by a Doctor or a Father of the Church or a pope, many of whom dedicated their lives to studying the meaning of Christ's gift to us, His divine words. Finally, the chapters conclude with modern reflections from men and women, sharing how that sacrament has graced and strengthened them in their lives today. May these moving essays by laymen and laywomen, consecrated religious, deacons, priests, and bishops encourage you and remind you what it means to be Catholic. Christ is forever faithful and never changes. Who are we that He has created us out of love, knit us in our mothers' wombs, called us by name, and asks us to be His earthly hands and feet? Let us all respond, "We, dear Lord, are and will remain Your faithful."

Introduction

My journey into the Catholic Church was very different from my children's. They were all baptized as infants and are surrounded by the Church's treasures in the sacraments at our local parish and in our devotions at home. This ecosystem of faith is not a mere coloring of things in holy crayons, but a true living and breathing of the life of grace as it has been given to us. The sacramental approach to life does not just use things to make stuff seem holy; rather, it senses and intuits the sacredness that impregnates the world, because just behind creation's veil is a loving Creator. My prayer as a father, of course, is that my children come to know Jesus Christ as their Lord and live vibrantly and virtuously in the Church He gave us, especially through the sacraments.

But my entrance into the Church was different, including how I received my first sacraments, because I converted as an adult. I had a conversion to Christ in my teenage years, believing in the basics of the gospel as they were presented by genuinely loving and faithful Protestants. But later, the sometimes chaotic divergence of belief among Protestants, the deep and traceable history of the Catholic Church, and the witness of Scripture all led me to knock on the door of a local Catholic parish. After that, I entered the Rite of Christian Initiation of Adults (RCIA). Unlike my children, I had to leave behind one community in order to join another, because the beliefs I held as a Protestant, though sharing much with Catholicism, were in uncompromising ways contradictory to it. There are some things in life that you can be at the same time, such as a policeman and a comic-book collector, and there are other things that are so different that to enter one requires leaving another, such as being single and being married. You simply cannot be both at the same time. And, like marriage, the Church marks the life-changing entrance into her membership with formal initiation, meaning a marked transition that is accompanied by rituals (the "rite" part of RCIA) and sacraments.

One of the graces of entering the Church as an adult is that I got to receive the Sacraments of Initiation

(Baptism, Confirmation, and the Eucharist) in the theological order that is inherent to them. Typically, because most of us know the order in which many children receive the sacraments, we think that Baptism is received in infancy, First Communion in childhood, and Confirmation in adolescence. There are historical reasons why this is the case today, but the actual order of those Sacraments—meaning their order when understood as the Sacraments of Initiation—is Baptism followed closely by Confirmation and then the Eucharist as the culmination. Walking through those sacraments in their true initiatory order helps us to see their coherence and deeper meaning. Many of us just see them as the first three in a list of seven, but in reality, they cannot be understood apart from one another, and to understand one, you must understand the rest and how they work together. In fact, the *Catechism* says that their "unity must be safeguarded" (*CCC* 1285). Really, to understand their power and purpose, we need to see them as a set, not in isolation.

How Initiation Happens

Helping one enter a new form of life is the very purpose in a true initiation. In the study of man (called anthropology), scholars have noted that there are typically three stages present in an initiation.[1] The first stage is a *separation* from the old life, often imaged as a form of death (i.e., the old life dying so the new life can "resurrect"). The second stage is the *transition*, wherein the threshold from old to new is crossed over and the new identity is fully revealed, received, and secured, or sealed. The last stage is *incorporation* into the community. This stage is largely ongoing, because the instruction in the new way of life cannot happen in an instant. Again, the very purpose and reason for an initiation is to help one cross over from individuality and an old way of life into life in the community that forms the new way of life. There are many important moments and experiences, but to

---

1 The authoritative text on the subject is Arnold Van Gennep's *The Rites of Passage*.

use the word "initiation" properly, all three of these stages should be recognizable.

Let us then look at each sacrament in its proper order (as most adults converts receive them), and see how they truly are best understood as a unity and form of initiation.

The Death

The first Sacrament of Initiation is Baptism, and this corresponds to the "death" of the old way of life that is a prerequisite for the new. The life of sin and the life of Christ are two different worlds, and we cannot peacefully live in both. "We have died, once for all, to sin," says St. Paul, "can we breathe its air again?" (Rom. 6:2, Knox). The waters of Baptism are not just a bath of cleansing; they are also a means of death. The waters in the font are both tomb and womb, and the latter requires the former. "We were buried therefore with him by baptism into death, so that as Christ was raised from the dead by the glory of the Father, we too might walk in newness of life" (Rom. 6:4).

Transition

The next stage of initiation is the transition, which corresponds to Confirmation. In many societies, the transition stage of initiation was when the new member was given a new or deeper identity, the tools associated with that identity, and the job he would perform within the body he was joining. For example, a medieval guild would bring in new members (often youths who had been in apprenticeship), give them their sets of tools, and position each within the village to exercise his craft as a "master" (a word that evolved into today's "Mister"). Knighthood, in fact, was a form of work in such a society, and the "tools" of the soldier (the sword, armor, etc.), were given to him at his knighting, a form of initiation.

In the life of grace, Confirmation also deepens our *filial identity*, meaning our life as God's children. And, as a sword is given to a knight, Confirmation gives us the tools we need to live that identity, and those tools point ultimately to the important job of all Christians, the worship of the Father. Through the sign of oil imparted on the forehead by a bishop, the sacrament truly seals our identity as Christians, a reality that is often signified by the taking of a new name at Confirmation. This outpouring of grace strengthens the Christian to live boldly and to exercise a sort of office (*quasi ex officio*) in regard to the public proclamation of the Gospel.[2] Confirmation cannot be understood without Baptism, because it brings to completion the life begun in Baptism. We become newborns in Baptism, but fully deputed Christians in Confirmation. As St. Thomas Aquinas says, "If one who is not baptized were to be confirmed, he would receive nothing," and he goes on to say, "Confirmation is to Baptism as growth to birth."[3]

In the office that comes through Confirmation, the Christian is given the unique "job" of praise, deputed in Christ for the perfect worship of the Father. In other words, Confirmation both perfects what came before (Baptism) and also points us to something else, the perfect worship of God and full incorporation into the life of Christ through the last Sacrament of Initiation.

Incorporation

The true spirit of initiation is very different from the obsession with our individual identities today, because initiation always points away from individuality toward a corporal existence, meaning the belonging that comes from membership in a body. The word "incorporation," after all, comes from the Latin *in corpus*, "into a body." Today we do the opposite, asserting the ego's rights above and before the good of the whole body. For the Christian, of course, the body we join is Christ's, which refers both to the Second Person of the Trinity in heaven and to His bodily presence on earth in the Church. But that

---

2 St. Thomas Aquinas, *Summa Theologica* (*STh*) III, 72, 5, ad 2.
3 St. Thomas Aquinas, *STh* III, 72, 6.

4 | SPIRIT AND LIFE

presence becomes even more intimate to us in the last Sacrament of Initiation, the Holy Eucharist. This is why Communion corresponds to the *incorporation* stage of initiation, because that's exactly what it does: it draws us further and further into the Church and into Christ, which are indistinguishable.

Unlike Baptism and Confirmation, which leave an indelible mark on the soul and can therefore be received only once, the Eucharist is something we receive many times, hopefully going deeper into its reality each time. The last stage of initiation—incorporation—is an ongoing stage, because we grow deeper and deeper into union with that to which we belong. For example, a man and woman are incorporated in marriage (they become, literally, one *body*, one *corpus*), but the act of incorporating, of growing in union, should go deeper and deeper and can reach only so far in the first days of marriage. So, too, our incorporation into Christ can go deeper each time we receive this sacrament. Therefore, although Baptism and Confirmation are long behind us, we can still say that this sacrament is one of initiation, even if ongoing, because we are being "conformed to the image of his Son" (Rom. 8:29).

The Need for Healing and Union

Yet, as any married couple knows, our fallen nature has a habit of trying to reclaim lost land. Sadly, "the new life received in Christian initiation has not abolished the frailty and weakness of human nature" (*CCC* 1426). We turn from our true loves for lesser or false ones. We sin. Sin causes an imbalance of justice, a wounding of relationship, and a disorder within the soul. In giving us the gift of the sacraments, Jesus was aware of our weakness, since, after all, He was like us in all things but sin (see Heb. 4:15). The God who watched as Adam and Eve gave up paradise for the lies of a serpent knows that we are prone to weaknesses and turning from the flowing waters of life to the putrid puddles of death. Because sin is never merely a wrong done in isolation, but a wrong done to a loving Father, it requires more than "setting things right" or even feeling better about ourselves. No, because it involves our relationship with God, others, and even ourselves, sin requires *healing*.

The Sacraments of Healing, commonly known as Confession and the Anointing of the Sick, show us the power of the Incarnation and the reality that God has created the body and even destined it for heaven, as we speak of in the Creed: "the resurrection of the body." The Anointing of the Sick has a beautiful simplicity to it. It is a petition of those who are weak in the flesh to the God who is generous to the spirit. We are not free from the effects of sin in this life; suffering and death are part of this valley of tears. Yet through this sacrament we receive not only the graces we need to face suffering but also the hope that God desires our healing, always interiorly and—if it is good for our souls—in our bodies. Facing physical suffering and death, we are not without the tangible comforts and strength of the sacramental life of the Church.

My wife and I faced a heavy cross of infertility early in our marriage. We found hope by discovering the problem, but it required surgery. The day before the surgery, my wife came down with an illness that could have prevented the surgery from occurring. Although it would have been postponed, this was very difficult because we longed so deeply for a baby. We called a priest for the Anointing of the Sick (which is common before surgery anyway), and after the anointing, the fever was lifted and the sickness ended immediately. Not all instances are as dramatic, but this was a wonderful sign that God does heal through His ministers and the sacraments entrusted to them.

Moving specifically to the life of the soul, the word "healing" helps us to understand the essentially spiritual aspect of Confession. We have all experienced wounds in our flesh and the processes required to heal them. One cannot continue the act that causes a wound, for example, and hope to be healed. Just so, to have a valid confession, one must have contrition—sorrow for the act and the firm purpose of turning

away from it in the future. As the degree of wounds worsens, so too the care they call for. Just so, while the confession of venial sins is helpful, as sin grips us tighter and tighter, or grows into the horror of mortal sin, tending the wound is no longer optional. As we saw, the Sacraments of Initiation draw us into belonging to Christ and His Church, but mortal sin is an offense so grave as to separate us from that Body. As a mortal wound can cause death if ignored, so a mortal sin can cause eternal death. All wounds do well in the care of a physician, especially those particularly grave ones. In the sacrament of Reconciliation—Confession—Christ Himself is the healer and physician, working through the priest. But in the case of mortal sin, the penitent is also appealing to the broader body for healing, and the priest, in a way, represents the entire body. In confessing mortal sins, we are reunited not only to God but also to His Body on earth through its earthly representative.

This brings us to the last two sacraments, which the *Catechism* says are "Sacraments at the Service of Communion." It also says they are "are directed toward the salvation of others" (1534). The devil's mission is to divide what ought to be united, but God draws all things together in Christ. He does this especially through the Sacraments of Matrimony and Holy Orders. Yes, marriage is a natural good practiced by non-Christians, but the Church has perennially taught that Christ Himself elevated marriage to the level of a sacrament, thereby offering special graces to those in this special union. Marriage is not only an image of Christ's love for the Church; it is also a witness of the power of communion. As a man who has been married since college, I know that (a) I am very different from my wife in her femininity, and that (b) I am literally incomplete without her. I need her in order to fully be and to understand myself as a husband and father. In Holy Matrimony I encounter and see visibly the fruitfulness of true love, especially in my children, and am assisted by the grace of a sacrament, which many couples ought to avail themselves of more often.

And while the sacrament of Marriage is an earthly image of the eternal love of God, Holy Orders directs us even more pointedly to our eternal destiny by drawing us close to it and by drawing eternity close to us. In marriage, nature draws forth more souls for God's kingdom, and in Holy Orders those souls are consecrated and sanctified for such a worthy kingdom. Since the first ordination at the Last Supper, there has been an unbroken ministerial priesthood that unites us to that first offering of the Mass and beckons us to the eternal banquet in heaven. Holy Orders is a sign and gift of God's goodness and is a constant source of comfort, for even in the face of scandal, error, and sin, the power of this sacrament stretches until the end of time and brings us the grace of God.

A Deep Desire

While it is easy to list our many challenges today, especially as regards living the faith in an increasingly hostile secular society, one we often overlook is the problem of isolation. We are a lonely and islanded people. It is true that consumerism is eating us, causing a frantic and unsatiated quest for the next and new thing, but part of the reason consumerism works is that we feel an emptiness that calls for filling. Humans were made by God to belong to one another, and to belong to Him. Let us not forget that right after the first sin of Adam and Eve, which separated them from God, Cain killed Abel, an image of our division from one another. Patricide precedes fratricide, and the two are always linked. It is in relationship to God and to each other that we understand who and what we are.

This is why I think that reorienting our understanding of the first three sacraments as what they are, Sacraments of Initiation, both clarifies our understanding of their unity and gives us a powerful tool in a lonely, metaphysically starving world. This sheds light on the coherence and logic of the others as well, so that we can see how wonderfully God has ordered His Church toward a mystical union on earth and in heaven. Men were made for belonging and for God. They need the sacred because they were made sacred. In other words, they long to be free from their ego's fickle desires and find a higher purpose, meaning, and place within the cosmos. They want freedom and healing. They want their sins forgiven. That cannot be done without a God who fulfills and a people who belong to one another. This is available fully in the Church. What we need is initiation, healing, and union. We don't need to take more pictures of ourselves and Tweet opinions. We need to be drawn out of ourselves, sealed in our true and lasting identity, and brought into a belonging that will not end, that reaches toward the eternity we hope for.

—Jason Craig

BAPTISM

CONFIRMATION

EUCHARIST

The Sacraments of Christian Initiation

The sacraments of Christian initiation—Baptism, Confirmation, and the Eucharist—lay the *foundations* of every Christian life. "The sharing in the divine nature given to men through the grace of Christ bears a certain likeness to the origin, development, and nourishing of natural life. The faithful are born anew by Baptism, strengthened by the sacrament of Confirmation, and receive in the Eucharist the food of eternal life. By means of these sacraments of Christian initiation, they thus receive in increasing measure the treasures of the divine life and advance toward the perfection of charity." (*CCC* 1212)

CHAPTER ONE

Baptism

Baptism as spoken about in

———

Sacred Scripture

Go therefore and make disciples of all nations, baptizing them in the name of the Father and of the Son and of the Holy Spirit, teaching them to observe all that I have commanded you; and lo, I am with you always, to the close of the age. —Matthew 28:19-20

Jesus answered, "Truly, truly, I say to you, unless one is born of water and the Spirit, he cannot enter the kingdom of God. That which is born of the flesh is flesh, and that which is born of the Spirit is spirit. Do not marvel that I said to you, 'You must be born anew.'"
—John 3:5-7

Catechism of the Catholic Church

Holy Baptism is the basis of the whole Christian life, the gateway to life in the Spirit, and the door which gives access to the other sacraments. Through Baptism we are freed from sin and reborn as sons of God; we become members of Christ, are incorporated into the Church and made sharers in her mission: "Baptism is the sacrament of regeneration through water in the word" (1213).

This sacrament is called *Baptism*, after the central rite by which it is carried out: to baptize (Greek *baptizein*) means to "plunge" or "immerse"; the "plunge" into the water symbolizes the catechumen's burial into Christ's death, from which he rises up by resurrection with him, as "a new creature." (1214).

This sacrament is also called *"the washing of regeneration and renewal by the Holy Spirit,"* for it signifies and actually brings about the birth of water and the Spirit without which no one "can enter the kingdom of God" (1215).

"This bath is called *enlightenment*, because those who receive this [catechetical] instruction are enlightened in their understanding . . . ." Having received in Baptism the Word, "the true light that enlightens every man," the person baptized has been "enlightened," he becomes a "son of light," indeed, he becomes "light" himself:

> Baptism is God's most beautiful and magnificent gift. . . . We call it gift, grace, anointing, enlightenment, garment of immortality, bath of rebirth, seal, and most precious gift. It is called *gift* because it is conferred on those who bring nothing of their own; *grace* since it is given even to the guilty; *Baptism* because sin is buried in the water; *anointing* for it is priestly and royal as are those who are anointed; *enlightenment* because it radiates light; *clothing* since it veils our shame; *bath* because it washes; and *seal* as it is our guard and the sign of God's Lordship. (1216)

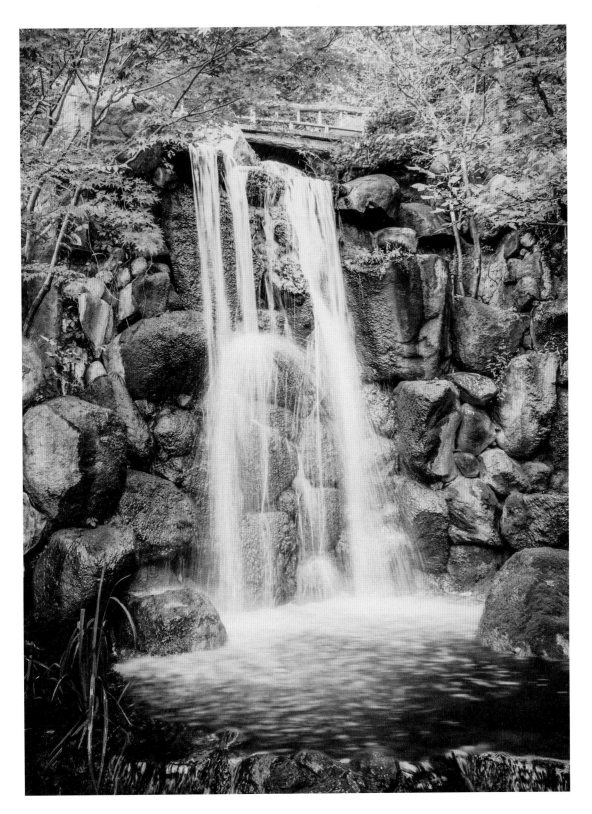

All the Old Covenant prefigurations find their fulfillment in Christ Jesus. He begins his public life after having himself baptized by St. John the Baptist in the Jordan. After his resurrection Christ gives this mission to his apostles: "Go therefore and make disciples of all nations, baptizing them in the name of the Father and of the Son and of the Holy Spirit, teaching them to observe all that I have commanded you" (1223).

By Baptism *all sins* are forgiven, original sin and all personal sins, as well as all punishment for sin. In those who have been reborn nothing remains that would impede their entry into the Kingdom of God, neither Adam's sin, nor personal sin, nor the consequences of sin, the gravest of which is separation from God (1263).

The Most Holy Trinity gives the baptized sanctifying grace, the grace of *justification*:
- enabling them to believe in God, to hope in him, and to love him through the theological virtues;
- giving them the power to live and act under the prompting of the Holy Spirit through the gifts of the Holy Spirit;
- allowing them to grow in goodness through the moral virtues. Thus the whole organism of the Christian's supernatural life has its roots in Baptism (1266).

Baptism makes us members of the Body of Christ: "Therefore . . . we are members one of another." Baptism incorporates us *into the Church*. From the baptismal fonts is born the one People of God of the New Covenant, which transcends all the natural or human limits of nations, cultures, races, and sexes: "For by one Spirit we were all baptized into one body" (1267).

Grace of Life

The Fall and its consequences. The redemptive grace of baptism.

In the beginning our God made man, so that, if he did not taste sin, he would not *surely die.* He committed sin, he became subject to death, he was driven out of Paradise. But the Lord, who wished his benefits to endure, who wished to destroy all the wiles of the serpent, and also to root out everything harmful, first gave sentence upon the man, *Earth thou art, and unto earth thou shalt go;* and he made man subject to death. It was a Divine sentence; it could not be paid by human means. A remedy was granted that man should die, and rise again. Why? In order that the thing which had been previously counted as a condemnation, might be counted as a benefit. What is that thing but death? Thou askest how. Because death intervening makes an end of sin. For when we die, we certainly cease to sin. Therefore, the sentence seemed satisfied, because man who had been made to live, on condition that he did not sin, was beginning to die. But, in order that the continual goodness of God might endure, man died, but Christ found the resurrection, that is, a way to restore the heavenly benefit which had been lost by the serpent's guile. Each, therefore, is for our good, since death is the end of sins, and the resurrection is the refashioning of our nature.

Nevertheless, that the craft or guile of the devil might not prevail in this world, baptism was devised. Concerning which baptism hear what the Scripture saith, nay, the Son of God, that *the Pharisees* who would not be *baptized with the baptism of John, rejected the counsel of God.* Therefore, baptism is the counsel of God. How great is the grace, where there is the counsel of God.

Hear, therefore. In order that the bands of the devil might be loosed in this world also, a means was found that man might die while living, and while living rise again. What is "living"? It is the living life of the body, when it came to the font, and was dipped into the font. What is water, but from the earth? Therefore, the heavenly sentence is satisfied without the insensibility which death brings. Thy dipping paid that sentence, *Earth thou art, and unto earth thou shalt go;* the sentence fulfilled, there is room for the heavenly benefit and remedy. So then, water is from the earth; Moreover the conditions of our life did not allow that we should be covered with earth, and rise from the earth; further, it is not earth, but water, that washes. Therefore the font is, as it were, a burial.

The threefold confession of faith and the threefold immersion in baptism described and explained. The unction after baptism.

Thou wast asked, "Dost thou believe in God the Father Almighty?" Thou saidst, "I believe," and didst dip, that is, thou wast buried. Again thou wast asked, "Dost thou believe in our Lord Jesus Christ, and in his Cross?" Thou saidst, "I believe," and didst dip; therefore, thou wast also *buried with Christ;* for he who is *buried with Christ,* rises again with Christ. A third time thou was asked, "Dost thou believe also in the Holy Ghost?" Thou saidst, "I believe," and didst dip a third time, that the triple confession might absolve the manifold fall of thy former life.

Thus (that we may give you an example), after the holy Apostle Peter seemed to have fallen during the Lord's passion by the weakness of human nature, he who had previously denied was afterwards thrice asked by Christ if he loved Christ, that he might cancel and annul that fall. Then he said, "*Thou knowest, Lord, that I love Thee.*" He said it thrice, that he might be thrice absolved.

Therefore, the Father forgives sin, just as the Son forgives; likewise also the Holy Ghost. But he bade us be baptized in one name, that is, *in the name of the Father, and of the Son, and of the Holy Ghost.* Wonder not that he spoke of one name, when there is one Substance, one Divinity, one Majesty. This is the name of which it was said, *Wherein* all *must be saved.* In this name ye have all been saved, ye have been restored to the *grace of life.*[1]

---

1   *St. Ambrose on the Mysteries and the Treatise on the Sacraments*, trans. T. Thompson, ed. J.H. Srawley (London: Macmillan, 1919), chap. 6, pars. 17-22.

A New Creation

Our lives are marked by two profound mysteries: birth and death. We are born in weakness and—no matter how beautiful, strong, or virile we may be—we return again to weakness.

Each day reminds us of these mysteries. We awake in the morning and are "born" anew. At night, we sleep and enter into a sort of death, lost entirely to the world of consciousness. The rhythm of birth and death, waking and sleeping defines the whole fabric of our lives. It is the life lived between these passages that defines who we become.

Birth and death are inescapable in the realm of matter. So too they define the reality of our spiritual lives, though, strange as it is to say, the process is inverted. We are all born suffering the fruit of Adam's sin and plagued by disordered passions and desires. We are at war with ourselves and others. But the most bitter fruit of all is death.

We were not made for death. It is foreign to the purpose of our creation. We were made for life, for full and intimate communion with God, who is Life itself. We were created to be temples of the living God, participants in His Being. The Holy Trinity dwelt within us in our original blessed state, penetrating every fiber of our being and renewing us at every moment. This was the source of our eternal life—drawing our vitality ceaselessly from the fountain of all Life, all Being, all Goodness, which is God Himself.

But the serpent deceived our original parents. He convinced them that they could live apart from God. "You will not die," were his words. He sowed the seeds of doubt; the lie of radical autonomy and self-sufficiency; the heresy that is the source of all others: that anyone or anything can live and thrive apart from communion with God.

Adam and Eve believed this lie. They disobeyed God, and in that moment the flow of living energy was cut off from them. They entered into spiritual death, and

their bodies, too, began slowly to die. Death and decay and disorder entered the world.

This spiritual death, this being cut off from grace and life, is the state in which we are all born. This is what the Church means by the stain of original sin; not that we are guilty of any actual sin when we are born, but rather that we experience "the privation of grace," as St. Thomas Aquinas explains. We are born in spiritual death, deprived of the grace of God. We are lamps with no light. We must find again the source of life. But how are we to do this? How can a dead man restore himself to life?

Christ revealed the answer when he spoke to Nicodemus. "Truly, truly, I say to you, unless one is born anew, he cannot see the kingdom of God" (John 3:3). The kingdom of God is life and light and immortality. Nicodemus, however, did not understand how a second birth was possible. He was thinking in physical terms and not spiritual. So Christ made the point again. "Truly, truly, I say to you, unless one is born of water and the Spirit, he cannot enter the kingdom of God" (John 3:5).

We are created suffering the effects of Adam's sin, cut off and deprived from God's life and in a state of spiritual death. We must be spiritually born anew. The life of God must surge again into our souls and breathe life into them. But how? The answer in Christ's words is clear: through water and the Holy Spirit. That is, through holy Baptism.

We must remember that Nicodemus was a Pharisee, a scholar dedicated to studying and teaching the law. He was well versed in the Scriptures, including the story of Creation. When he heard the words "water and the spirit," he undoubtedly called to mind the words of the second verse in the first chapter of Genesis: "The earth was without form and void, and darkness was upon the face of the deep; and the Spirit of God was moving over the face of the waters." It was of creation that Christ spoke—the creation of the world, yes, but also the new creation of a spiritual soul.

What a profound mystery! The restoration of a soul to spiritual life is as phenomenal as the creation of the world, or perhaps more so. In Baptism, it is as if Christ speaks His creative Word to the soul, as He did at the dawn of time, calling it from nothingness into being, from death into life, through the power of the Holy Spirit.

In the *Rite of Baptism*, the priest explicitly states that at the dawn of Creation, the Holy Spirit breathed on the waters and made them the wellspring of all holiness. The priest then asks the Father and the Son to send the Holy Spirit upon the water in the baptismal font and asks that all who are buried with Christ in the death of Baptism may rise with him to newness of life. The life and light of God Himself, the energy of His divine grace, floods into our souls in Baptism, vivifying them and energizing them. Our sins are washed away, and we are intimately united to Christ, drawing our life and sustenance from Him as a branch does from a vine. We are restored to friendship and communion with God and once again share in His eternal life, as we were created to do.

St. Paul describes this passage from death into life beautifully: "Therefore, if any one is in Christ, he is a new creation; the old has passed away, behold, the new has come" (2 Cor. 5:17). A baptized Christian, then, is as fresh and new and wondrous as the world on the first day of creation.

The life of grace in our souls is a tremendous gift. It is a spiritual inheritance that even angels envy. But Baptism is not an end; it is a beginning—the beginning of the profound adventure that is the spiritual life. With the great gift of salvation comes a great responsibility. We must keep the fire of grace burning in our souls. We must not let it be extinguished through lukewarmness, indifference, or sin. Many dangers will threaten us. Temptations and trials will be our constant companions. But he who is faithful to the end will be saved.

As Catholics, we should rejoice in our Baptism and frequently call to mind the baptismal promises we made. We should also jealously guard the grace we have been given, for it is a precious treasure. In short, let us heed well this exhortation, taken from the traditional *Rite of Baptism*, and so find eternal life:

> Receive this burning light, and keep thy Baptism so as to be without blame: keep the commandments of God, that when the Lord shall come to the nuptials, thou mayest meet Him together with all the Saints in the heavenly court, and mayest have eternal life and live for ever and ever.

———

Jack Michael

I was recently walking along Elysian Fields Avenue in New Orleans when the faint sound of a brass band echoed through the live oak trees. The music rose to a crescendo, and church doors swung open. Pallbearers carrying a somber casket slowly made their way out. People flooded behind, dancing, crying, and waving white handkerchiefs. I watched as the priest gave the final blessing and cast a splash of holy water that landed gently on the casket. It was a compelling reminder of Baptism.

As St. Paul wrote to the Romans, "We were indeed buried with him through baptism into death, so that, just as Christ was raised from the dead by the glory of the Father, we too might live in newness of life" (Rom. 6:4). As the hearse departed up the rumbling street, the chorus of funeral goers began to sing: "O Lord, I want to be in that number when the saints go marching in."

The time between Baptism and death is typically a blurry, expansive jumble. It involves years of discovery, connection, celebration, and suffering. Yet, these two events in our lives mark what is most essential and most certain. They become our identity, our mission, and our surrender. As a dear professor shared, "At our conception we receive all that we are as a sheer gift. And at our death we return every offering. These bookends frame the meaning of everything between. Life, if lived in faith, should synthesize these two into perfect harmony. Gift received, gift offered back." Through the Baptism and death of my infant son, Jack Michael, I became a part of his offering.

Jack's Baptism was unlike those of my other children, who received the sacrament in magnificently adorned historical churches. We were just four. My husband and I, Jack, and Fr. Daniel in the hospital NICU, separated from the other patients by a simple curtain. Jack lay motionless in his isolette surrounded by tubes and beeping monitors. Fr. Daniel's hand, massive in comparison with Jack's body, tenderly applied the oil of salvation to his chest. "May you have strength in the power of Christ our Savior." Sobbing, I gripped

my husband's hand and reminded myself to breathe. I pictured Mary standing at the foot of the Cross. How did she do it? I needed her strength.

Closing my eyes, I remembered the circumstances that led up to this moment. From the earliest weeks of my pregnancy, Jack and I were bonded. I recalled nights of uncertainty, pain, bleeding, and constant prayer. I thought of that time I woke up at the hospital knowing exactly what name to give him and the many letters I wrote to him. On January 24, I saw Jack for the first time. He was a tiny, two-pound miracle. Two weeks passed, and each day in the NICU, I held Jack, kissed him, and celebrated every ounce he gained. "Jack Michael, I baptize you in the name of the Father, the Son and the Holy Spirit." By the world's standards, a little one whose life is marked by suffering does not make sense. Indeed, it's a source of anger. Yet, as I faced Jack's death, I felt peace. Jack's identity and mission came into crystal-clear focus. He was grafted to the vine. He was hidden in Christ's wounds.

Emerging anew after being plunged into the depths, Jack's life bore witness to the entire purpose of the Christian life. From St. Paul, "We are afflicted in every way, but not constrained; perplexed, but not driven to despair; persecuted, but not abandoned; struck down, but not destroyed; always carrying about in the body the dying of Jesus, so that the life of Jesus may also be manifested in our body" (2 Cor. 4:8-10). Jack's quiet surrender came five days after he was baptized. I held him in my arms as he breathed his last. I went to Mass at a church called Mater Dolorosa. Behind the altar was a striking image of Mary, Mother of Sorrows, holding Jesus after He was taken down from the Cross. Mary's eyes were bloodshot and puffy with dark circles underneath. Gazing on the image, I wanted to take everything back. The initial strength I felt melted away in the burden of recognized grief. I felt broken, the way she appeared. I was desperate for Jack to be safe in my arms again. Soon after that, Jesus answered my plea. As the priest held up the Eucharist, I felt him saying, "Take my body instead."

The day of Jack's funeral, a flood hit New Orleans. Local schools cancelled afternoon classes due to the threat of rising waters. The uptown streets were saturated. A song lyric played in my mind, "Even when the rain falls, / Even when the flood starts rising, / Even when the storm comes, / I am washed by the water." I stood up to give Jack's eulogy and looked out upon so many faces of friends and family members who had weathered the storm beside us. They had been our shelter for many months. Jack had opened up a precious vulnerability inside me. I recognized that opening myself to offers of support allowed me to identify more deeply in the Body of Christ.

I held my older son's hand as I walked down the aisle to exit the church. We followed closely behind my husband, who carried Jack's tiny casket with tears streaming down his face. Fr. Daniel met us to offer a final blessing of holy water as Jack's body was driven away. In the distance, we could hear the faint sounds of a piano playing slowly and beautifully, "O Lord, I want to be in that number when the saints go marching in." Through his Baptism, I knew that Jack had joined that number with Mary taking over as his mother.

Several months later, we found out that I was expecting another baby. The due date was no coincidence. Easter Sunday.

CHAPTER TWO

Confirmation

Confirmation as spoken about in

———

Sacred Scripture

While Apollos was at Corinth, Paul passed through the upper country and came to Ephesus. There he found some disciples. And he said to them, "Did you receive the Holy Spirit when you believed?" And they said, "No, we have never even heard that there is a Holy Spirit." And he said, "Into what then were you baptized?" They said, "Into John's baptism." And Paul said, "John baptized with the baptism of repentance, telling the people to believe in the one who was to come after him, that is, Jesus." On hearing this, they were baptized in the name of the Lord Jesus. And when Paul had laid his hands upon them, the Holy Spirit came on them; and they spoke with tongues and prophesied. —Acts 19:1-6

Catechism of the Catholic Church

Baptism, the Eucharist, and the sacrament of Confirmation together constitute the "sacraments of Christian initiation," whose unity must be safeguarded. It must be explained to the faithful that the reception of the sacrament of Confirmation is necessary for the completion of baptismal grace. For "by the sacrament of Confirmation, [the baptized] are more perfectly bound to the Church and are enriched with a special strength of the Holy Spirit. Hence they are, as true witnesses of Christ, more strictly obliged to spread and defend the faith by word and deed" (1285).

In the Old Testament the prophets announced that the Spirit of the Lord would rest on the hoped-for Messiah for his saving mission. The descent of the Holy Spirit on Jesus at his baptism by John was the sign that this was he who was to come, the Messiah, the Son of God. He was conceived of the Holy Spirit; his whole life and his whole mission are carried out in total communion with the Holy Spirit whom the Father gives him "without measure" (1286).

This fullness of the Spirit was not to remain uniquely the Messiah's but was to be communicated to *the whole messianic people.* On several occasions Christ promised this outpouring of the Spirit, a promise which he fulfilled first on Easter Sunday and then more strikingly at Pentecost. Filled with the Holy Spirit the apostles began to proclaim "the mighty works of God," and Peter declared this outpouring of the Spirit to be the sign of the messianic age. Those who believed in the apostolic preaching and were baptized received the gift of the Holy Spirit in their turn (1287).

From this fact, Confirmation brings an increase and deepening of baptismal grace:
- it roots us more deeply in the divine filiation which makes us cry, "Abba! Father!";
- it unites us more firmly to Christ;
- it increases the gifts of the Holy Spirit in us;
- it renders our bond with the Church more perfect;

- it gives us a special strength of the Holy Spirit to spread and defend the faith by word and action as true witnesses of Christ, to confess the name of Christ boldly, and never to be ashamed of the Cross:

> Recall then that you have received the spiritual seal, the spirit of wisdom and understanding, the spirit of right judgment and courage, the spirit of knowledge and reverence, the spirit of holy fear in God's presence. Guard what you have received. God the Father has marked you with his sign; Christ the Lord has confirmed you and has placed his pledge, the Spirit, in your hearts (1303).

Like Baptism which it completes, Confirmation is given only once, for it too imprints on the soul an *indelible spiritual mark*, the "character," which is the sign that Jesus Christ has marked a Christian with the seal of his Spirit by clothing him with power from on high so that he may be his witness (1304).

This "character" perfects the common priesthood of the faithful, received in Baptism, and "the confirmed person receives the power to profess faith in Christ publicly and as it were officially... (1305).

Every baptized person not yet confirmed can and should receive the sacrament of Confirmation. Since Baptism, Confirmation, and Eucharist form a unity, it follows that "the faithful are obliged to receive this sacrament at the appropriate time," for without Confirmation and Eucharist, Baptism is certainly valid and efficacious, but Christian initiation remains incomplete (1306).

Anointed

Having been *baptized into Christ*, and *put on Christ* (Gal. 3:27), you have been made conformable to the Son of God; for God having *foreordained us unto adoption as sons* (Eph. 1:5), made us *to be conformed to the body of Christ's glory* (Phil. 3:21). Having therefore become *partakers of Christ* (Heb. 3:14), you are properly called Christs, and of you God said, *Touch not My Christs*, or anointed. Now you have been made Christs, by receiving the antitype of the Holy Ghost; and all things have been wrought in you by imitation, because you are images of Christ. He washed in the river Jordan, and having imparted of the fragrance of His Godhead to the waters, He came up from them; and the Holy Ghost in the fullness of His being lighted on Him, like resting upon like. And to you in like manner, after you had come up from the pool of the sacred streams, there was given an Unction, the anti-type of that wherewith Christ was anointed; and this is the Holy Ghost; of whom also the blessed Esaias, in his prophecy respecting Him, said in the person of the Lord, *The Spirit of the Lord is upon Me, because He has anointed Me: He has sent Me to preach glad tidings to the poor* (Isa. 61:1).

For Christ was not anointed by men with oil or material ointment, but the Father having before appointed Him to be the Saviour of the whole world, anointed Him with the Holy Ghost, as Peter says, *Jesus of Nazareth, whom God anointed with the Holy Ghost* (Acts 10:38). David also the Prophet cried, saying, *Your throne, O God, is for ever and ever; a sceptre of righteousness is the sceptre of Your kingdom; You have loved righteousness and hated iniquity; therefore God even Your God has anointed You with the oil of gladness above Your fellows*. And as Christ was in reality crucified, and buried, and raised, and you are in Baptism accounted worthy of being crucified, buried, and raised together with Him in a likeness, so is it with the unction also. As He was anointed with an ideal oil of gladness, that is, with the Holy Ghost, called oil of gladness, because He is the author of spiritual gladness, so you were anointed with ointment, having been made partakers and *fellows of Christ*.

But beware of supposing this to be plain ointment. For as the Bread of the Eucharist, after the invocation of the Holy Ghost, is mere bread no longer, but the Body of Christ, so also this holy ointment is no more simple ointment, nor (so to say) common, after invocation, but it is Christ's gift of grace, and, by the advent of the Holy Ghost, is made fit to impart His Divine Nature. Which ointment is symbolically applied to your forehead and your other senses; and while your body is anointed with the visible ointment, your soul is sanctified by the Holy and life-giving Spirit.

And you were first anointed on the forehead, that you might be delivered from the shame, which the first man who transgressed bore about with him everywhere; and that *with unveiled face ye might reflect as a mirror the glory of the Lord.* (2 Corinthians 3:18) Then on your ears; that you might receive the ears which are quick to hear the Divine Mysteries, of which Esaias said, *The Lord gave me also an ear to hear* (Isa. 50:4); and the Lord Jesus in the Gospel, *He that has ears to hear let him hear* (Matt. 11:15). Then

on the nostrils; that receiving the sacred ointment ye may say, *We are to God a sweet savour of Christ, in them that are saved* (2 Cor. 2:15). Afterwards on your breast; that having *put on the breast-plate of righteousness,* you may *stand against the wiles of the devil.* For as Christ after His Baptism, and the visitation of the Holy Ghost, went forth and vanquished the adversary, so likewise ye, after Holy Baptism and the Mystical Chrism, having put on the whole armour of the Holy Ghost, are to stand against the power of the adversary, and vanquish it, saying, *I can do all things through Christ which strengthens me* (Phil. 4:13).

Having been counted worthy of this Holy Chrism, you are called Christians, verifying the name also by your new birth. For before you were deemed worthy of this grace, you had properly no right to this title, but were advancing on your way towards being Christians.

Moreover, you should know that in the old Scripture there lies the symbol of this Chrism. For what time Moses imparted to his brother the command of God, and made him High-priest, after bathing in water, he anointed him; and Aaron was called Christ or Anointed, evidently from the typical Chrism. So also the High-priest, in advancing Solomon to the kingdom, anointed him after he had bathed in Gihon (1 Kings 1:39). To them however these things happened in a figure, but to you not in a figure, but in truth; because you were truly anointed by the Holy Ghost. Christ is the beginning of your salvation; for He is truly the First-fruit, and you the mass (Romans 11:16); but if the First-fruit be holy, it is manifest that Its holiness will pass to the mass also.

Keep this unspotted: for it shall teach you all things, if it abide in you, as you have just heard declared by the blessed John, discoursing much concerning this Unction. For this holy thing is a spiritual safeguard of the body, and salvation of the soul. Of this the blessed Esaias prophesying of old time said, *And on this mountain*—(now he calls the Church a mountain elsewhere also, as when he says, *In the last days the mountain of the Lord's house shall be manifest* [Isa. 2:2])—*on this mountain shall the Lord make unto all nations a feast; they shall drink wine, they shall drink gladness, they shall anoint themselves with ointment.* And that he may make you sure, hear what he says of this ointment as being mystical; *Deliver all these things to the nations, for the counsel of the Lord is unto all nations.* Having been anointed, therefore, with this holy ointment, keep it unspotted and unblemished in you, pressing forward by good works, and being made well-pleasing to the Captain of your salvation, Christ Jesus, to whom be glory for ever and ever. Amen.[1]

---

1 St. Cyril of Jerusalem, Catechetical Lecture 21.

Confirmation Reflection by Matthew Samson

———

The Commissioning

"For though we live in the world, we are not carrying on a worldly war, for the weapons of our warfare are not worldly, but have divine power to destroy strongholds (2 Corinthians 10:4)."[1]

When we think of wars, the first thing that comes to mind are probably those that involve countries fighting over land, resources, or power. Do we ever take the time to realize that we are fighting our own war every day of our lives? We are all members of the Church Militant, which is the body of Christian believers on earth. We are all members of God's army here on earth. We are fighting a war, not for worldly things, but for souls.

In any army, soldiers must be trained and equipped with weapons in order to do battle. God does not send His soldiers into battle without preparing them. In Confirmation, the Holy Spirit bestows on us the weapons we need to confront our foe. These weapons are the gifts of wisdom, understanding, counsel, fortitude, knowledge, piety, and fear of the Lord. The word "Confirmation" comes from the Latin roots *con*, which means "together," and *firmare*, which means "to strengthen." God uses this sacrament to bring together and strengthen His warriors for battle. After receiving this sacrament, one has put on a full suit of armor of the Holy Spirit. It's like being commissioned as an officer after training. Officers are commissioned to lead others into battle and to come out on the other end successful. We are infused with the gifts of the Spirit so that we might lead ourselves and others to become members of the Church Triumphant.

Model Soldier of Christ

I was confirmed when I was twelve years old. The saint I chose to be with me on that special day was St. Martin of Tours. I chose him because his life was very inspiring to me. Although St. Martin left the Roman army, he never stopped fighting for what he

---

1 Paul Thigpen, *Manual for Spiritual Warfare* (Charlotte, NC: TAN Books, 2014), 35.

believed in. He left his Roman commanding officers to fight for the King of the universe. He left the crest of his legion and accepted the insignia of the Cross. In Confirmation, we receive the insignia of the Cross on our foreheads.

When I received Confirmation, I wanted to become a soldier of some sort when I grew up. As I grew older, I began to pursue another career path. I wanted to obtain a college degree in business and become a successful businessman. I obtained the degree I wanted, and I worked at a job that I believed would help me achieve my goal. Just when I thought everything I had planned was coming to fruition, I received an invitation for something I never would have imagined. Regretfully, as I pursued my career and worldly interests, I let my prayer life fall by the wayside. I grew dull in my faith life. My faith never left me, but by my actions one could ascertain that it was not my highest priority. I was not winning the battle as a member of the Church Militant. In my heart, I knew that I was pursuing a career that would not ultimately satisfy

me, but I did not know what I was supposed to do with my life.

The Blessed Mother at My Side

I decided to ask the Blessed Mother for help. As I prayed, I told her that I knew I was not on the right path, but I didn't know which path to choose. That night, I had a dream in which I asked for her assistance and was shown that I was to fight evil with her help.

I know that dreams can be deceiving, so after this occurred, I sought counsel. I also knew after this that I wanted to live my life for the Blessed Mother. Before I could pursue anything, I knew that I had to make changes in my life. Mary put on my heart a desire to pray the Rosary. By means of the Rosary, Eucharistic Adoration, and attending Daily Mass, I slowly started to shake off the snares that had bound me and began to suit up with armor again. This transition led me to consecrate my life to Mary. I will never forget that

day when I entrusted myself totally to her. I gave up trying to pursue my own path and accepted whatever she has planned for me. It was after this that doors started to open.

I eventually discerned, with the help and guidance of many people, that I should enter the seminary. This is not a decision that I could have chosen on my own. The advice and counsel of many people helped me to see that, ultimately, it is not what I want, but what God wants. Once I surrendered my plans, I started to see more clearly where He was leading me.

While I was discerning whether I should enter the seminary, the idea of becoming a military chaplain kept coming to my attention. I decided to ask for help from someone whom I had been so fond of when I was younger, St. Martin of Tours. Little did I know that the Confirmation saint I had chosen when I was twelve would become so prominent in my prayer life. After additional discernment, I decided that someday I wanted to become a military chaplain.

St. Martin of Tours once cut his cloak in two and gave half to a shivering beggar. That night, Martin had a dream of Christ wearing the half cloak that he had given to the beggar and thanking Martin for his generosity. What about the other half of the cloak, which St. Martin kept for himself? It was preserved and venerated as a relic after St. Martin's death. The person in charge of caring for this relic was called a *cappellanus*. This Latin term translated into Old French is *chapelain*. Today we use the word "chaplain." When I chose St. Martin of Tours to be my Confirmation saint, I did not expect my choice to become so meaningful. I now constantly pray for his intercession in my endeavors. I feel as if we should all embody the strength with which St. Martin of Tours so bravely defended the Faith.

Equipped for Spiritual Battle

By his life, St. Martin of Tours set the bar high, but we can all hope to achieve this strength. We have the necessary weapons, given to us by the Holy Spirit in

Confirmation. The *Catechism of the Council of Trent* teaches that after being confirmed, one "becomes stronger with the strength of a new power, and thus begins to be a perfect soldier of Christ." It also teaches that through the Sacrament of Confirmation, the Holy Spirit "infuses Himself into the souls of the faithful, and increases in them strength and fortitude to enable them, in the spiritual contest, to fight manfully and to resist their most wicked foes."[2]

One can see the importance of Confirmation. We are being called to join and become commissioned in the Church Militant for the salvation of our souls and the souls others. Confirmation is the perfection of our union into this body. The gifts we receive in Confirmation help us not to be afraid to evangelize to souls. We must never be ashamed of proclaiming the truth of Christ.

"In the Holy Spirit we have from God a mighty Ally and Protector, a great Teacher of the Church, a mighty Champion on our behalf. We must not be afraid of the demons, nor of the Devil himself; for more powerful than those is the One who fights for us. But we must open our doors to Him, *for He goes about seeking those who are worthy* and searching for those on whom He may bestow His gifts."[3]

---

2 Ibid., 50.

3 St. Cyril of Jerusalem, quoted in ibid., 128.

—

The Soldiers of Jesus Christ

The only thing I remember from my Confirmation is choosing St. Joan of Arc to be my Confirmation saint. I selected her because leading an army and getting burned at the stake seemed a lot cooler to me than living a quiet life and dying a quiet death in a convent, like so many of the saints with whom I was familiar. I still have a great devotion to the example and intercession of St. Joan of Arc, but I like to think that these days, I have a better understanding of *why* I do.

It's because of Joan's willingness to do God's will rather than because of her remarkable political and military successes that I should admire her. After all, God can work wonders through the most unlikely of people.

Just look at the disciples. They spend their days learning from Jesus Himself. They watch Him perform miracle after miracle. They are sent out to perform miracles themselves. And yet, somehow, they totally don't get it. It's like the secret comic relief of the Bible. There they are, with Jesus and the four thousand, and the disciples ask, "Where are we to get bread enough in the desert to feed so great a crowd?" (Matt. 15:33).

And all of *us* are thinking, "Umm . . . maybe the same place you got it two chapters ago when it was five thousand people." They know Jesus, but they don't understand Him.

They react with fear when He sends the demons into the swine, and with amazement when He arrives to heal Jairus's daughter, and with bewilderment in almost every other instance, whether He's teaching in the temple or healing a paralytic and a deaf man.

But the disciples of the Acts of the Apostles are a different story completely.

One minute, they are hapless, confused, worried, and unable to understand stuff that Jesus says right to their faces, and the next, they are starting the Church, spreading the gospel across the globe, and enduring hardship, slander, and martyrdom like hero geniuses.

Peter the fisherman explains Scripture and converts thousands with a single homily. The same men who argued among themselves over who would be the

greatest come together to work out the first major crisis of the young Church and decide to support bacon for all. Of the ten apostles who fled in fear on the night of Jesus' arrest, each eventually goes boldly to his martyrdom. Seven of the next eight popes follow suit.

So what's the pivot point? It's Pentecost, when the Holy Spirit descends upon the apostles and Mary in the upper room and changes everything (Acts 2:1-4).

It's the gifts of the Holy Spirit that we see at work in the Acts of the Apostles. Wisdom, understanding, counsel, fortitude, knowledge, piety, and fear of the Lord replace the disciples' former identifying traits of confusion, misunderstanding, and fear of miracles.

And, good news for the rest of us: God, through the Catholic Church, has given us the same "special outpouring of the Holy Spirit as once granted to the apostles on the day of Pentecost" (*CCC* 1302) in the sacrament of Confirmation.

Confirmation, Baptism, and the Eucharist constitute the Sacraments of Initiation. Our Confirmation "confirms" and completes the graces given to us at our Baptism and is renewed in our reception of the Eucharist. With it, the baptized, "are more perfectly bound to the Church and are enriched with a special strength of the Holy Spirit. Hence they are, as true witnesses of Christ, more strictly obliged to spread and defend the faith by word and deed" (*CCC* 1285)—and also by suffering and the pen if you're St. Paul; by banner and sword if you're St. Joan of Arc; by littleness and self-control if you're St. Thérèse; and by small children and Instagram if you're me.

It is our Confirmation that gives us the ability and the obligation to witness to Christ in this crazy, mixed-up world of ours in every generation.

In the Confirmation ceremony in the Roman Rite, the bishop extends his hands over those receiving the sacrament. Since the time of the apostles, this gesture has signified the gift of the Spirit. The bishop invokes the outpouring of the Holy Spirit in these words:

"All-powerful God, Father of our Lord Jesus Christ,
by water and the Holy Spirit
you freed your sons and daughters from sin
and gave them new life.
Send your Holy Spirit upon them
to be their helper and guide.
Give them the spirit of wisdom and understanding,
the spirit of right judgment and courage,
the spirit of knowledge and reverence.
Fill them with the spirit of wonder and awe in your presence.
We ask this through Christ our Lord" (CCC 1299).

Christ's gift of the Holy Spirit to His people has built up His Church to prevail against the gates of hell, against the Arian heresy, scoundrel popes, schism and revolt, postconciliar upheavals, and even the scandals of today. Through the grace of the sacrament of Confirmation, Christ raised up the great saints of the patristic age and the monastic age and the Counter-Reformation to reform and get through those profound troubles.

He is raising up saints among us today. I got to see it firsthand last summer in the Sackcloth and Ashes movement, when (at least) hundreds of thousands of Catholics from all over the world came together over a hashtag that a friend and I created to meet scandal and tragedy with prayer, fasting, and acts of reparation.

People who had never fasted, fasted. People who didn't regularly pray, prayed daily for forty days. People who were themselves victims of abuse felt heard and loved and supported. Everyday Catholics felt less powerless. Jesus' Merciful Heart was consoled (I hope).

For me, the forty days was the most committed I had ever been to prayer, fasting, and reparation. I could see the good fruit it bore in my life, in my family, and in my community. It made me realize that the long tradition of penance practiced by generations of Catholics before us is not, perhaps, quite as outdated and unnecessary as I had heard.

It was the Holy Spirit working through us in the medium of our age—social media—to create support and community in a time of crisis in the Church. It's through the graces of the Holy Spirit at Confirmation and the saints of the Internet age that the Catholic Church will continue to outlast her enemies.

The *Baltimore Catechism* says that Confirmation "is the sacrament through which the Holy Ghost comes to us in a special way and enables us to profess our faith as strong and perfect Christians and soldiers of Jesus Christ" (330). It's one of my favorite images. How amazing to consider ourselves part of something bigger than ourselves: soldiers working together toward individual and common goals, each using our particular gifts to advance the cause. Each empowered by the Holy Spirit.

Come, Holy Spirit, fill the hearts of your faithful and kindle in them the fire of your love. Send forth your Spirit, and they shall be created. And You shall renew the face of the earth.

O, God, who by the light of the Holy Spirit, did instruct the hearts of the faithful, grant that by the same Holy Spirit we may be truly wise and ever enjoy His consolations. Through Christ Our Lord. Amen.

By our Confirmation, we are strong and perfect Christians. We are soldiers of Jesus Christ. By our Confirmation, we are equipped to suffer for our Faith. By our Confirmation, we have a responsibility to share and defend our Catholic Faith. By our Confirmation, we are charged with using our particular strengths to help bring about the kingdom. By our Confirmation, we can try crazy, great things.

As my friend St. Joan of Arc is said to have said, "Act, and God will act. Work, and He will work."

GLORIA IN EXCELSIS DE

CHAPTER THREE

Eucharist

Eucharist as spoken about in

Sacred Scripture

Truly, truly, I say to you, he who believes has eternal life. I am the bread of life. Your fathers ate the manna in the wilderness, and they died. This is the bread which comes down from heaven, that a man may eat of it and not die. I am the living bread which came down from heaven; if any one eats of this bread, he will live forever; and the bread which I shall give for the life of the world is my flesh.

The Jews then disputed among themselves, saying, "How can this man give us his flesh to eat?" So Jesus said to them, "Truly, truly, I say to you, unless you eat the flesh of the Son of man and drink his blood, you have no life in you; he who eats my flesh and drinks my blood has eternal life, and I will raise him up at the last day. For my flesh is food indeed, and my blood is drink indeed. He who eats my flesh and drinks my blood abides in me, and I in him. As the living Father sent me, and I live because of the Father, so he who eats me will live because of me. This is the bread which came down from heaven, not such as the fathers ate and died; he who eats this bread will live forever." —John 6:47-58

———

Catechism of the Catholic Church

The holy Eucharist completes Christian initiation. Those who have been raised to the dignity of the royal priesthood by Baptism and configured more deeply to Christ by Confirmation participate with the whole community in the Lord's own sacrifice by means of the Eucharist (1322).

"At the Last Supper, on the night he was betrayed, our Savior instituted the Eucharistic sacrifice of his Body and Blood. This he did in order to perpetuate the sacrifice of the cross throughout the ages until he should come again, and so to entrust to his beloved Spouse, the Church, a memorial of his death and resurrection: a sacrament of love, a sign of unity, a bond of charity, a Paschal banquet 'in which Christ is consumed, the mind is filled with grace, and a pledge of future glory is given to us'" (1323).

The Eucharist is "the source and summit of the Christian life." "The other sacraments, and indeed all ecclesiastical ministries and works of the apostolate, are bound up with the Eucharist and are oriented toward it. For in the blessed Eucharist is contained the whole spiritual good of the Church, namely Christ himself, our Pasch" (1324).

In the communion, preceded by the Lord's prayer and the breaking of the bread, the faithful receive "the bread of heaven" and "the cup of salvation," the body and blood of Christ who offered himself "for the life of the world" (Jn. 6:51):

> Because this bread and wine have been made Eucharist ("eucharisted," according to an ancient expression), "we call this food *Eucharist*, and no one may take part in it unless he believes that what we teach is true, has received baptism for the forgiveness of sins and new birth, and lives in keeping with what Christ taught" (1355).

We must therefore consider the Eucharist as:
- thanksgiving and praise to the *Father*;
- the sacrificial memorial of *Christ* and his Body;

- the presence of Christ by the power of his word and of his *Spirit* (1358).

To the offering of Christ are united not only the members still here on earth, but also those already *in the glory of heaven*. In communion with and commemorating the Blessed Virgin Mary and all the saints, the Church offers the Eucharistic sacrifice. In the Eucharist the Church is as it were at the foot of the cross with Mary, united with the offering and intercession of Christ (1370).

The Council of Trent summarizes the Catholic faith by declaring: "Because Christ our Redeemer said that it was truly his body that he was offering under the species of bread, it has always been the conviction of the Church of God, and this holy Council now declares again, that by the consecration of the bread and wine there takes place a change of the whole substance of the bread into the substance of the body of Christ our Lord and of the whole substance of the wine into the substance of his blood. This change the holy Catholic Church has fittingly and properly called transubstantiation" (1376).

The unity of the Mystical Body: the Eucharist makes the Church. Those who receive the Eucharist are united more closely to Christ. Through it Christ unites them to all the faithful in one body—the Church. Communion renews, strengthens, and deepens this incorporation into the Church, already achieved by Baptism. In Baptism we have been called to form but one body. The Eucharist fulfills this call: "The cup of blessing which we bless, is it not a participation in the blood of Christ? The bread which we break, is it not a participation in the body of Christ? Because there is one bread, we who are many are one body, for we all partake of the one bread" (1396).

His Words

Who then is the author of the sacraments but the Lord Jesus? From heaven those sacraments came, for all counsel is from heaven. But it was truly a great and divine miracle that God *rained down manna* from heaven, and the people ate without toiling.

Thou sayest perhaps, "My bread is of the usual kind." But that bread is bread before the words of the sacraments; when consecration has been added, from bread it becomes the flesh of Christ. Let us therefore prove this. How can that which is bread be the body of Christ? By consecration. But in what words and in whose language is the consecration? Those of the Lord Jesus. For all the other things that are said in the earlier parts of the service are said by the priest: praises are offered to God, prayer is asked for the people, for kings, and the rest; when it comes to the consecration of the venerable sacrament, the priest no longer uses his own language, but he uses the language of Christ. Therefore, the word of Christ consecrates this sacrament.

What is the word of Christ? That, to be sure, whereby all things are made. The Lord commanded, and the heaven was made; the Lord commanded, and the earth was made; the Lord commanded, and the seas were made; the Lord commanded, and every creature was produced. Thou seest, therefore, how effective is the word of Christ. If, therefore, there is such power in the word of the Lord Jesus, that the things that were not began to be, how much more is it effective that things previously existing should, without ceasing to exist, be changed into something else? The heaven was not, the sea was not, the earth was not; but hear David saying, *He spoke, and they were made: he commanded, and they were created.*

Therefore, that I may answer thee, it was not the body of Christ before consecration; but after consecration, I tell thee, it is now the body of Christ. *He spoke, and it was made: he commanded, and it was created.* Thou thyself didst formerly exist, but thou wast an old creature; after thou wast consecrated, thou didst begin to be a new creature. Wilt thou know how thou art a new creature? *Everyone,* it says, *in Christ is a new creature.*

Hear, then, how the word of Christ is wont to change every creature, and changes, at will, the ordinances of nature. In what way? thou askest. Hear; and, first of all, let us take an example from his generation. It is usual that a man is not generated save from a man and a woman and the use of marriage; but because the Lord willed it, because he chose this mystery, Christ was born of the Holy Spirit and the Virgin, that is, *the mediator between God and men, the man Christ Jesus*. Thou seest, then, that he was born contrary to the ordinances and course of nature; he was born as man from a virgin.

Hear another example. The people of the Jews were hard-pressed by the Egyptians; they were shut in by the sea. At the divine command, Moses touched the waters with his rod, and the wave divided, certainly not according to the use of its own nature, but according to the grace of the heavenly command. Hear another. The people thirsted; they came to the spring. The spring was bitter; holy Moses *cast wood* into the spring, and the spring that had been bitter was made sweet; that is, it changed the use of its nature and received the sweetness of grace.

From all these examples, then, dost thou not understand how effectual is the heavenly word? If the heavenly word was effectual in the earthly spring, if it was effectual in other things, is it not effectual in the heavenly sacraments? Therefore, thou hast learnt that what was bread becomes the body of Christ, and that wine and water are put into the chalice but become blood by the consecration of the heavenly word.

But perhaps thou sayest, "I do not see the appearance of blood." But it has the likeness; for as thou hast taken *the likeness of the death*, so also thou drinkest the likeness of the precious blood, that there may be no shrinking from actual blood, and yet the price of redemption may effect its work. Thou hast learnt, therefore, that what thou receivest is the body of Christ.

But that thou mayest know that this is a sacrament, it was prefigured beforehand. Then learn how great is the sacrament. See what he says: *As often as ye do this, so often will ye make a memorial of me until I come again.*

And the priest says: "Therefore, having in remembrance his most glorious passion and resurrection from the dead and ascension into heaven, we offer to thee this spotless offering, reasonable offering, unbloody offering, this holy bread and cup of eternal life: and we ask and pray that thou wouldst receive this oblation on thy altar on high by the hands of thy angels, as thou didst vouchsafe to receive the presents of thy righteous servant Abel, and the sacrifice of our patriarch Abraham, and that which the high priest, Melchizedek offered to thee."

Therefore as often as thou receivest—what saith the Apostle to thee?—as often as we receive, we show the Lord's death; if we show his death, we show remission of sins. If, as often as blood is poured forth, it is poured for remission of sins, I ought always to receive it, that my sins may always be forgiven me. I, who am always sinning, ought always to have a remedy. Therefore, thou hast come to the altar, thou has received the body of Christ. Hear again what sacraments thou hast obtained. Hear holy David speaking. He too foresaw these mysteries in the spirit and rejoiced and said that he *lacked nothing*. Why? Because he who hath received the body of Christ shall never hunger.

How often hast thou heard the twenty-third Psalm and not understood? See how it is suited to the heavenly sacraments. *The Lord is my shepherd; and I shall not want. In a green pasture, there hath he made me to lie down. He hath tended me by the water of comfort, he converteth my soul. He hath led me in the paths of righteousness for his name's sake. Yea, though I walk through the valley of the shadow of death, I will fear no evil, for thou art with me. Thy rod and thy staff, they have comforted me.* Rod is rule, staff is passion; that is the eternal Divinity of Christ, but also his passion in the body. The one created, the other redeemed.

Thou hast prepared a table before me against them that trouble me. Thou hast anointed my head with oil, and my inebriating cup, how glorious it is.

Therefore, thou hast come to the altar, thou hast received the grace of Christ, thou hast obtained the heavenly sacraments.[1]

---

1 *St. Ambrose on the Mysteries and the Treatise on the Sacraments*, trans. T. Thompson, ed. J. H. Srawley (London: Macmillan, 1919), chaps. 3, 4, 6, pars. 12–20, 26–28.

Sacred Exchange

"This is *my Body*…This is the chalice of *my Blood*…"

For a moment, I felt as if I couldn't believe what I was hearing. These words were, of course, the words of consecration—the miraculous and sacred words of Jesus Himself first spoken on the night before His Passion—finding their way from that Upper Room, having transcended time and place and language, and here and now being pronounced at this sacrosanct moment in the Mass, bearing the one and the same power by which the bread and the wine truly become His Body and Blood. Yet, at this instant, it was a particular detail that caused me to be astounded as never before: the voice sounding those sublime words.

Stooping over the altar was my friend, who had just been ordained a priest the day before—and this was his first offering of the Mass. Perhaps it was the familiarity of the voice as those words were being pronounced that struck me: the voice of someone who was more or less the same age as I, whom I'd gotten to know and journey with these past years in the seminary. The voice of someone whom I at times

have both admired and been proud of and, at other times, have been disappointed and frustrated with. Maybe it was more that latter part that beckoned something in me in that split second to deliberate, "Wait—is this really happening?" And yet, it really was…there was my friend Nathan: *in persona Christi*—"in the person of Christ."

I should mention where I was (spatially) during that moment of consecration. I was kneeling right before the altar, not more than a few feet away. It was a new vantage point for me as well, having just been ordained earlier that week (in my case, as a transitional deacon.)[1] I was honored when he asked me a year earlier that, Lord willing, I serve as a deacon at his first Mass. Leading up to this moment, we'd done as much as we could in our poor way to prepare: we fasted and prayed, begging God and the intercession of His saints: the Blessed Mother, our own patron saints, and holy priests such as St. John Vianney and St. Padre Pio to help us hone our minds, direct our

---

1   A deacon preparing for the priesthood.

souls, and purify our hearts as we anticipated these great mysteries of the sacrament of Holy Orders and the Holy Sacrifice of the Mass. Outside our liturgy classes, we practiced the movements and gestures, reflected on the text, and recited the chants on our own. The more we did, the recognition of the reality that one day it would be the "real one" became greater and greater. Yet, as we exhaustively rehearsed, there was one part we had always left off: the words of consecration. Perhaps it's over-romanticizing things a bit, but it didn't seem or feel appropriate to rehearse those words. When we arrived at that part during our preparation outside class, those words were just not said, and the resulting obvious vacuity was almost overbearing.

Fast-forward to that first Mass; to that moment of consecration; clear enough for me to hear: *This is my Body…This is the Chalice of my Blood…Do this in memory of me.* Even though my ordination had happened a few days before, it wasn't until then—at that moment, upon hearing my friend speak those words and believing that the bread and wine were truly transformed into the Body and Blood of Christ— that I realized: things were definitely not going to be the same anymore. The fact that we were there, having been placed, through a series of events, and no doubt, by the magnanimity of God into these new roles, was for me, a personal Eucharistic "miracle."

It was as if I were seeing for the first time and from a new perspective—spiritually and quite literally— what happens in the part of the Mass known as the Liturgy of the Eucharist. There, Jesus, through the hands of His priest, takes bread and wine, and by the Holy Spirit and through His words of consecration, changes them into His Body and Blood as He makes an offering of Himself to the Father. There is a parallel of transformation between these offerings of bread and wine and the situation I found myself in at that moment. In the ceremonious offering of the bread and wine in the Offertory just a few moments prior are symbols that we sometimes miss. We offer the "fruit of the earth and work of human hands": bread and wine that come from God's creation and tell the story of seasons having passed, and through our labor, God allows us to imprint ourselves on this offering.

What is offered is our collective toil and work, our tears and sweat, our small sacrifices, but, with that, our history and culture, our anthropology, indeed our wider humanity, and our time—our aging and our mortality. These we can offer, in our lowliness, out of God's creation, from His provision, for, in His magnanimity, He doesn't leave us to come empty-handed! Nestled within that story of the wider human journey was my own personal trek and the series of events that have passed in my life leading to this moment. And now what we've offered have been transformed into Christ's Body and Blood, which He offers to the Father as an acceptable sacrifice and gives back to us the Bread of Life and the Cup of Salvation.

In recognizing this sacred exchange of offering, partaking, and accepting, I can best appreciate the mystery of vocation—and in my case, the vocation to the priesthood and my current diaconate. In other words, the Eucharist helps me ease me from the mentality of "I have nothing to offer God" to the recognition that I, too—that is, my journey, my being, my poor self-offering, albeit in a different manner—can be considered "fruit of the earth and work of human hands."

By "fruit of the earth," I mean that I too, realizing that I am a part of His creation, have God to thank for my existence—for the miracle of my life! I can humbly give God praise in that, as the psalmist says, "[He] knit me together in my mother's womb … fearfully and wonderfully made … when I was woven together in the depths of the earth" (Ps 139:14-15).

I realize that by God's providence and grace, I grew up, was educated, matured, and am now the man I am thanks in part to interactions with others and the sacrifices of others; shaped by joys and disappointments, triumphs and failures; influenced by living teachers and by the collective wisdom of human history, good and bad—in other words, the "work of human hands."

And all these would still fall short of being the acceptable sacrifice if it weren't for Jesus, who receives all of these from our hands and, taking them into His holy and venerable hands, places them on the altar of sacrifice, and by the Holy Spirit, makes of them a perfect offering to the Father: Himself. He would not have it any other way. *Do this in memory of me.*

As my friend celebrated Mass that day, I realized that indeed, for me, things were not going to be the same anymore…as on a sacramental level, I was not to be the same anymore. Humbled, I marveled at the fact that I am a deacon, whereas once I was not. I reflected on how the bread and wine are changed forever, yet they retain the appearances and qualities of bread and wine. And just so, I realized that I too was changed forever, yet I still retain my qualities, my personality, even my defects and weaknesses. Through ordination, I've received not superpowers but a gift of a hidden configuration to Christ the Servant and, with it, the delicate responsibilities of faithfully living that *diakonia* in its countless manifestations and taking

upon myself the identity of "the one who serves" (Luke 22:27). Only in His name and by the mandate of His Church am I to carry out *His* ministry "with humility and love in order to assist the bishop and the priests and to serve [His people]."[2] Before anticipating ordination to the priesthood, my ordination to the diaconate was a mandate to proclaim and preach the Gospel with my voice and deeds, and so to learn to "believe what you read, teach what you believe, and practice what you teach."[3]

As I knelt there as a deacon during that Mass (and at every Mass I've served at since), I couldn't help but shudder to think that there I was in the Upper Room and, at the same time, kneeling at the foot of the Cross—that here we are before the source and summit of our Christian lives, and in those familiar words we truly hear the Risen Jesus Himself saying, "This is *my Body*… This is the chalice of *my Blood*…"

---

2   Rite of Ordination of a Deacon.
3   Ibid.

Eucharist Reflection by Kelly J. Henson

———

Heart Speaks unto Heart

I was in fifth grade, and my frequent searches for craft materials sent me ever deeper into the recesses of our basement storage area. A weathered picture frame caught my eye. As I gently eased the yellowed print out into the dusty light from the exposed bulb overhead, the luminous image arrested my attention. There was Jesus, looking calm, authoritative, and welcoming, and on His chest was a burning, bleeding heart. My family had just converted to the Catholic faith, and the Sacred Heart was quite different from the religious imagery I had seen before. Why could I see His heart? Why was it burning? Where did we get this picture? My dad explained to me that this image used to hang above my beloved Catholic grandma's bed when she was young. And He had been waiting for me all this time until the right moment.

As I added other Catholic sacraments and devotions to the Christian faith I had grown up with and loved, this picture became my own icon of a deepening knowledge of the Person of Christ. I received my first Holy Eucharist later that fall, tears brimming in my eyes, and I began to grasp that this great sacrament was nothing less than the Heart of Christ, offered for me and to me for no other reason than Love. The Heart of Christ is both literal and symbolic, because He is both fully human and fully divine. In His humanity, Jesus allowed His flesh to be beaten and pierced for our sins. The water and blood that flowed from His side completed the offering He raised to the Father at the Last Supper, transforming simple bread and wine. Yet, because He is also fully divine, the symbol of His Heart represents the fullness of His divine nature, especially as the personification of Love.

As a young adult, through daily Mass and adoration, I began to appreciate how the Mass itself brings us to an authentic understanding of the Eucharistic Lord. When I arrived at the church with a chaotic mind and troubled heart, I would walk up the aisle to my seat flanked by the Stations of the Cross, reminding me that I never need suffer alone. As the Mass began, I encountered the Word of God leading me, like one of the disciples on the road to Emmaus, through the loyalty of the Father to His chosen people, into the mystery of the Word made incarnate in the Gospels

and in the Creed, where I had the privilege to bow my head in reverence and reaffirm my trust in the Savior of the World.

Every time I try to encompass God with my mind, I discover that it is impossible to describe the ardor of the Divine Heart that reaches out to me. He shatters my expectations and strides through my heart with His flame of love to illuminate every corner and reveal my misguided attempts to achieve happiness and fulfillment on my own. Attentive to my limited insight, Jesus unfolds His love to me one radiant facet at a time, so that I may learn to see the brilliance of His Presence everywhere through that new lens.

We need help to rise above the doldrums of ordinary life and into the realm of the spirit. The comforting discipline of ritual accomplishes this transformation through words more ancient and profound than our own. But what sets the Catholic Mass apart from every secular ritual or hopeful devotion, every appeal for life-giving rain and every lullaby against the dark, is the Liturgy of the Eucharist, in which we encounter a living Person who is both the source and summit of our lives.[1]

Six years ago, I knelt on the cold floor of a school auditorium as the Host was held aloft a moment after the words of consecration hummed over the nodding heads of sleepy students. I too was fighting fatigue, since pregnancy and lingering nausea sapped my energy. Suddenly, I felt a flutter, a leap, in my core. It was the first time I had felt this little soul, and she was springing like John the Baptist in seeming acknowledgment of her hidden Lord. I knew that the same jubilant recognition should enflame my own heart every time my Savior is lifted before my eyes. Eucharist means "thanksgiving" (*CCC* 1360), and we should yearn to cry out in praise as Our Lady did in her Magnificat at the incredible gift of a Lord who desires to dwell with us and within us.

---

1 *Lumen Gentium* (*LG*), no. 11.

Yet sometimes we struggle to stay awake even one hour with our Lord (Matt. 26:40). We grow confused when we hope for a feeling of transformation and are left with a nagging sense that maybe we would have "done it all better" if it hadn't been for the man whose nose was whistling one pew away from ours. Thankfully, the Mass is not a graded performance. Some days we may come with an abundance to offer our Lord, and sometimes we will arrive with a widow's mite (Mark 12:41-44) or a few loaves and fishes (Matt. 14:17). God asks nothing less at the Offertory than our very selves, frail as we may be. Through our reception of the Eucharist, He steps past the realm of the senses, even past the fickle realm of the emotions, and communes directly with our hearts. This communion of heart speaking to heart[2] through His Presence in the Eucharist—Body, Blood, Soul, and Divinity—is the greatest manifestation of Christ's human and divine love for each one of us. This quiet gaze of Love is the fulfillment of the promise He made to be "with you always, to the close of the age" (Matt. 28:20).

If the incredible gift of Confession sets me free from the shackles of sin, then the Eucharist is what I am freed *for*. We are invited to shed anxiety, addiction, laziness, lust, envy, pride, falsehood, and every other vice that promises comfort but results in empty pain. In its place, Christ extends the cup that holds the saving blood and living waters flowing from His pierced side: peace despite pain, love despite loneliness, faithful guidance amid the chaos of this world, and joy eternally. Do we truly believe He will fulfill His promises? When He asks us, "Who do you say that I am?" (Matt. 16:15), do we hesitate? Perhaps, like Eve in the garden, we are suspicious of His desire to give us all that is good for us. Or, like Judas, we may desire a change in our circumstances more than an interior transformation through the school of suffering and humility. We fear the cost of love; after all, on the crucifix we can see what love cost Him.

---

2 From the motto on the coat of arms chosen by John Henry Cardinal Newman.

To be in relationship with God, there must be a response to His eternal outpouring of selfless love. Pope Benedict XVI says, "The Eucharist draws us into Jesus' act of self-oblation … into the very dynamic of his self-giving."[3] As Christ says, "This is my body, which is given for you" (Luke 22:19), we should respond in kind. And in this way, the great mystery of Christ's redeeming sacrifice is also the portal through which He can enter into the most mundane aspects of our lives. No humble sacrifice accepted for His sake is too little; no whispered "I love you" misses the attentive ears of this Lover.

A pernicious lie that can nag at the edges of our prayer is the feeling that we are not actually called to the intimacy with God that the saints enjoy. We think that maybe religious nuns or bishops or particularly holy, retired people are called to the highest levels of communion with God, but not we busy, ordinary people who still struggle to be patient with the least

disappointment in our day. This is another miracle of the Eucharistic love; the Eucharist is the same for every person who receives Our Lord. In each Host is the complete gift of Jesus. If we can begin working to empty ourselves of vice and selfishness, we will make room in our hearts to receive Him. He would fill us to overflowing with a purity of love beyond any earthly love we have experienced. This is the universal call to holiness.[4] Every one of us is perpetually invited to begin anew to choose heroic love, a love that will renounce lower things for the sake of that which is better. And like children on the seashore who toss aside a chipped shell in favor of a flawless one, our movement toward Beauty will only increase our desire to ask for more of His grace and intimacy.

Christ offers Himself to be consumed so that we may be consumed by His Love. If you seek Him, you will find Him[5]—as a still voice in the wilderness, as a

---

3 *Deus Caritas Est*, no. 13.

4 *LG*, no. 40.
5 Matt. 7:7-8.

small child, as a humble carpenter, as a healer, as a teacher, as a warrior triumphant over evil and death, and as a God aflame with love for you. In receiving the Eucharist, each of our hearts is made a tabernacle for His Heart, and we carry Him forth to heal our broken world. May He help us to be worthy of the gift of being Christ-bearers to others, for it is our greatest joy and our salvation.

PENANCE

ANOINTING OF THE SICK

The Sacraments of Healing

Through the sacraments of Christian initiation, man receives the new life of Christ. Now we carry this life "in earthen vessels," and it remains "hidden with Christ in God." We are still in our "earthly tent," subject to suffering, illness, and death. This new life as a child of God can be weakened and even lost by sin. (*CCC* 1420)

The Lord Jesus Christ, physician of our souls and bodies, who forgave the sins of the paralytic and restored him to bodily health, has willed that his Church continue, in the power of the Holy Spirit, his work of healing and salvation, even among her own members. This is the purpose of the two sacraments of healing: the sacrament of Penance and the sacrament of Anointing of the Sick. (*CCC* 1421)

CHAPTER FOUR

Penance

Penance as spoken about in

———

Sacred Scripture

"If you forgive the sins of any, they are forgiven; if you retain the sins of any, they are retained." —*John 20:23*

"All this is from God, who through Christ reconciled us to himself and gave us the ministry of reconciliation; that is, God was in Christ reconciling the world to himself, not counting their trespasses against them, and entrusting to us the message of reconciliation. So we are ambassadors for Christ, God making his appeal through us. We beseech you on behalf of Christ, be reconciled to God." —*2 Corinthians 5:18-20*

Catechism of the Catholic Church

"Those who approach the sacrament of Penance obtain pardon from God's mercy for the offense committed against him, and are, at the same time, reconciled with the Church which they have wounded by their sins and which by charity, by example, and by prayer labors for their conversion" (1422).

It is called the *sacrament of conversion* because it makes sacramentally present Jesus' call to conversion, the first step in returning to the Father5 from whom one has strayed by sin.

It is called the *sacrament of Penance*, since it consecrates the Christian sinner's personal and ecclesial steps of conversion, penance, and satisfaction (1423).

It is called the *sacrament of confession*, since the disclosure or confession of sins to a priest is an essential element of this sacrament. In a profound sense it is also a "confession"—acknowledgment and praise—of the holiness of God and of his mercy toward sinful man.

It is called the *sacrament of forgiveness*, since by the priest's sacramental absolution God grants the penitent "pardon and peace."

It is called the *sacrament of Reconciliation*, because it imparts to the sinner the love of God who reconciles: "Be reconciled to God." He who lives by God's merciful love is ready to respond to the Lord's call: "Go; first be reconciled to your brother" (1424).

Only God forgives sins. Since he is the Son of God, Jesus says of himself, "The Son of man has authority on earth to forgive sins" and exercises this divine power: "Your sins are forgiven." Further, by virtue of his divine authority he gives this power to men to exercise in his name (1441).

"The whole power of the sacrament of Penance consists in restoring us to God's grace and joining us with him in an intimate friendship." Reconciliation with God is thus the purpose and effect of this sacrament. For those who receive the sacrament of Penance with contrite heart and religious disposition, reconciliation "is usually followed by peace and serenity of conscience with strong spiritual consolation." Indeed the sacrament of Reconciliation with God brings about a true "spiritual resurrection," restoration of the dignity and blessings of the life of the children of God, of which the most precious is friendship with God (1468).

———

Cry of Reflection

In God Alone Is the Hope and Joy of Man

Let me know You, O Thou who know me; let me know You, as I am known (1 Cor. 13:12). O Thou strength of my soul, enter into it, and prepare it for Yourself, that You may have and hold it without spot or wrinkle (Eph. 5:27). This is my hope, therefore have I spoken; and in this hope do I rejoice, when I rejoice soberly. Other things of this life ought the less to be sorrowed for, the more they are sorrowed for; and ought the more to be sorrowed for, the less men do sorrow for them. For behold, You desire truth, seeing that he who does it comes to the light (John 3:20). This wish I to do in confession in my heart before You, and in my writing before many witnesses.

That All Things Are Manifest to God; that Confession unto Him Is Not Made by the Words of the Flesh, but of the Soul, and the Cry of Reflection

And from You, O Lord, unto whose eyes the depths of man's conscience are naked (Heb. 4:13), what in me could be hidden though I were unwilling to confess to You? For so should I hide You from myself, not myself from You. But now, because my groaning witnesses that I am dissatisfied with myself, Thou shinest forth, and satisfiest, and art beloved and desired; that I may blush for myself, and renounce myself, and choose You, and may neither please You nor myself, except in You. To You, then, O Lord, am I manifest, whatever I am, and with what fruit I may confess unto You I have spoken. Nor do I it with words and sounds of the flesh, but with the words of the soul, and that cry of reflection which Your ear knows. For when I am wicked, to confess to You is naught but to be dissatisfied with myself; but when I am truly devout, it is naught but not to attribute it to myself, because Thou, O Lord, bless the righteous; but first Thou justify him ungodly (Rom. 4:5). My confession, therefore, O my God, in Your sight, is made unto You silently, and yet not silently. For in noise it is silent, in affection it cries aloud. For neither do I give utterance to anything that is right unto men which You have not heard from me before, nor do You hear anything of the kind from me which Yourself said not first unto me.

He Who Confesses Rightly unto God Best Knows Himself

What then have I to do with men, that they should hear my confessions, as if they were going to cure all my diseases? A people curious to know the lives of others, but slow to correct their own: Why do they desire to hear from me what I am, who are unwilling to hear from You what they are? And how can they tell, when they hear from me of myself, whether I speak the truth, seeing that no man knows what is in man, save the spirit of man which is in him? (1 Cor. 2:11). But if they hear from You anything concerning themselves, they will not be able to say, "The Lord lies." For what is it to hear from You of themselves, but to know themselves? And who is he that knows himself and says, "It is false," unless he himself lies? But because charity believes all

things (1 Cor. 13:7) (among those at all events whom by union with itself it makes one), I too, O Lord, also so confess unto You that men may hear, to whom I cannot prove whether I confess the truth, yet do they believe me whose ears charity opens unto me.

But yet do Thou, my most secret Physician, make clear to me what fruit I may reap by doing it. For the confessions of my past sins—which You have forgiven and covered, that You might make me happy in You, changing my soul by faith and Your sacrament—when they are read and heard, stir up the heart, that it sleep not in despair and say, I cannot; but that it may awake in the love of Your mercy and the sweetness of Your grace, by which he that is weak is strong (2 Cor. 12:10), if by it he is made conscious of his own weakness. As for the good, they take delight in hearing of the past errors of such as are now freed from them; and they delight, not because they are errors, but because they have been and are so no longer. For what fruit, then, O Lord my God, to whom my conscience makes her daily confession, more confident in the hope of Your mercy than in her own innocency—for what fruit, I beseech You, do I confess even to men in Your presence by this book what I am at this time, not what I have been? For that fruit I have both seen and spoken of, but what I am at this time, at the very moment of making my confessions, various people desire to know, both who knew me and who knew me not—who have heard of or from me—but their ear is not at my heart, where I am whatsoever I am. They are desirous, then, of hearing me confess what I am within, where they can neither stretch eye, nor ear, nor mind; they desire it as those willing to believe—but will they understand? For charity, by which they are good, says unto them that I do not lie in my confessions, and she in them believes me.[1]

---

1   *Confessions*, bk. 10, chaps. 1-3.

—————

Return to Me

It might sound odd for me to claim that Confession is one of my favorite sacraments, but how could it not be when I have found such tremendous mercy and redemption in it?

If I am merciful to others in my ministry and teaching settings, it is because I have been shown great mercy. More than once, I have been the prodigal son who runs off with the wealth and blessings of the Father, waking up later in my filth and empty self-centeredness, only to return to the open arms of a God who knows and loves me with reckless abandon.

One of our Faith's greatest treasures is the sacrament of mercy itself, Reconciliation, commonly called Confession. Now, I could point to the establishment of this sacrament from the early Church councils, reference writings of the Church Fathers, elaborate on Scripture's encouraging us to confess our sins (1 John 1:9) and gave His apostles the power to loose and bind sins (Matt. 18:18), but I prefer to share with you the awe and appreciation I have for this holy mystery.

Confession has proven to be the steadfast reminder of my fallenness and need for the mercy of God in order to run well this earthly race.

A God of Grit and Grime

I realize that my love of Confession seems like a strange notion in our modern time. To confess anything implies that I committed a wrong. In our relativistic times, in which there is supposedly no objective truth and "sin" is a lost concept, can anything be wrong? Does sin even exist anymore?

To go before a priest in Confession and personally, bodily, and vulnerably own up to my sins certainly stands in sharp contrast to the airbrushed and flawless facade I'm expected to keep up online. We live in an age of disconnection, in which we can hide behind phone screens and digital barriers and block anything uncomfortable. We can manicure our social media presence to make sure we're portrayed as spotless with the perfect filters. We can delete our flaws, block

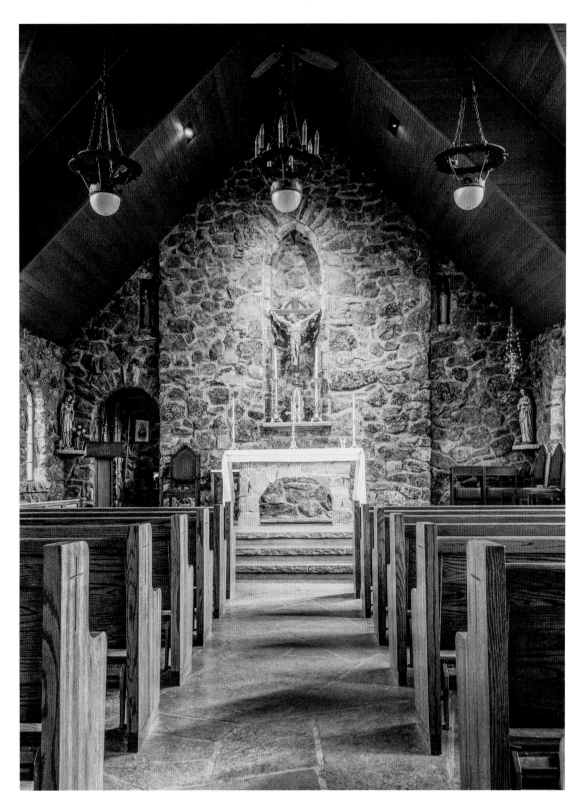

annoyances, and delete browser histories so we look as if we have nothing to hide.

But there's a problem. We're not perfect. We all have things that we hide.

I know that I'm broken and wounded. I've felt the weight of sin on my soul, the compounded effects of lust, anger, self-centeredness, and spiritual laziness. I'm tempted to lie and steal. I've allowed myself to be in unhealthy relationships, driven by lust and insecurity. I'm immensely prone to sin. That's not being neurotic; it is an honest diagnosis of the problem at hand. We can't receive healing without first naming the disease.

There's a human need to repent and conform ourselves to what is true. More often today, we attempt to do so through incomplete, imperfect and even distorted means, such as therapy and reveal-all moments on daytime talk show. People post way-too-revealing details of their lives online because of a sincere need for human connection and for the truth to be known. We desire to be seen and loved for the wholeness of who we are, no matter how we try to bury the details.

Religious or not, we have an instinctive revulsion to liars and to being lied to. We value men and women of integrity who walk uprightly, whose behavior matches their talk. Immoral actions done in secret eat away at us because we're living in darkness. We desire the truth and to live in the light of truth. The truth sets us free and brings healing.

The beauty, of course, is that through Jesus Christ we are offered far more than a cathartic moment on a talk show: we are offered a real return to the wholeness for which we have been made. Jesus is the Truth that can dispel our falsities and infirmities, but only if we first confess that we have a need to be healed.

Often when Jesus encountered the sick, He would bring healing to the soul just as readily as to the body. When men brought their paralyzed friend to Jesus to be healed, Jesus first forgave the man's sins (Matt. 9:1-8). The Apostle James encouraged the sick, "Confess your sins to one another and pray for another, that you may be healed" (James 5:16). Confession brings a *real* interior and exterior healing.

Only God can forgive sins, of course. The Pharisees were horrified when Jesus claimed the authority to forgive sins, because He was essentially equating himself with Yahweh, the God of Abraham, Isaac, and Jacob. Such a claim intimated the fantastic idea that God would deign to take on crude flesh to live in our grit and grime and walk among us.

That was precisely what God deigned and did.

Returning to the Father

Hours before we were married, my wife and I went to Confession separately, wanting to enter into marriage as free as we could be. We confessed times when we gave away our love to individuals who didn't deserve it and times when we ourselves failed to love as we should. I knew that through years of viewing pornography, I had given myself to so many other women, but that through God's grace my mind and memory had begun the healing process. On our wedding day, we wanted to come together without any reservation of our past and be intimately one. And that's what Confession is all about.

The word "Reconciliation" emphasizes a return to intimacy with God. The hint of spousal love is not accidental; it is exactly the point. God wants us to be present with Him in each moment with that level of spousal unity. Sin isn't the mere breaking of a rule, but the severing of a loving relationship. Confession is the rightful movement back to the Divine Lover, who longs for our return.

"Return, Israel, to the Lord your God," said the prophet Hosea to his people in exile (Hos. 14:2). Time and time again, the Hebrew people forgot the goodness of the Lord, and yet God stood steadfast as only a lover could. Time and time again, we are tempted to walk away from the Lord's goodness, yet God waits on our return. Through the imperfect priest, we are given access to the Perfect Lover of our souls.

Pope Francis stated that it's not God who tires of forgiving us, but we who tire of asking for forgiveness. I know that I experienced shame and frustration with having to return to the sacrament week after week for issues of lust in my college years. I would go to different parishes, worried that the priests would start remembering me. Of course, I was missing the point that I needed to be held accountable and that God was always, always waiting there in the priest to receive me back into that intimate relationship with Him.

Now that I'm a parent, my children, of course, do things that try my patience and push me to anger. My anger with them lasts but a moment, and in the next instant, I try to console, reconcile and shower love on them. God the Father sees us with such infinite love that no sin we ever commit can separate us from Him. But we must be humble enough to say, "Forgive me, Father, for I have sinned."

Go and Sin No More

The answer to the moral crises of our time is to live in holiness. In every time of trial for the Church, great saints have risen to lead the response, souls humble enough to admit that they are sinners in need of a Savior.

At the end of each confession, we say an Act of Contrition, in which we assert our intent to avoid whatever leads us into sin. There is a danger of treating Confession as a quick car wash when we frequent the sacrament without committing to changing problematic behaviors and habits. This cheapens the divine mercy God offers us through the blood of Christ.

How serious are we about living this call to repentance? We must be "all in." We must be willing to get to the roots of our habits and to see where our wounds originated. "If your eye causes you to sin, pluck it out" (Mark 9:47). I have friends who have downgraded their phones to "dumb phones," so that they could be free of their endless temptations to lust, envy, and sloth. I installed software on my computer years ago to help me overcome pornography use and hold me accountable, for the sake of my soul and my future vocation. It's not easy, and it takes time. But through our examining the origins of our scars, God is glorified and we can be transformed. Behaviors can be corrected and wholeness can be achieved with the assistance of the Divine Healer.

Pardon and Peace

"For freedom Christ has set us free" (Gal. 5:1). God did not send His only Son so that we might have more rules and live in fearful, neurotic guilt, but that we might have life in abundance (John 10:10). A life lived in the divine love and truth will truly set us free.

I try to go to Confession at least once a month. St. John Paul II would go once a week—what the pope had to confess, only God knows! The holier we become, the more we see our selfish tendencies and flaws and see the great distance between who we are and who we could be. The great saints attest to this fact. But still God pours His grace out upon those humble enough and persistent enough to ask for it.

Experience the healing God wants to pour out upon you. Return to the intimacy of God in this treasured sacrament of the Church. Confess and believe in the glory of God!

—

Joy and Mercy

Confession and pizza: that was a common Saturday-evening combination for the Armour family. When my dad would say, "Get ready, kids. We're going to Confession tonight," the reaction would be squeals of delight and a frenzy of bustling to get ready because we all knew what came after Confession: an all-you-can-eat buffet at a local pizza place that included yummy dessert pizza and endless fountain drinks. This tradition instilled in us from an early age a decidedly positive association with the sacrament of Confession. Freedom from sin was seen as something to celebrate. And it made perfect sense to my mind as a child because, well, if heaven throws a party over one repentant sinner, why shouldn't we? But in our version of the prodigal son story, instead of celebrating by feasting on a fatted calf, we feasted on pizza.

As a religious sister, I have been blessed to encounter many families who are creating similar traditions for their children in the practice of Confession. One family with four girls began the custom of buying a special necklace for their daughters on the occasion of their First Reconciliation as a sign of what happens at that moment: God restoring the soul's beauty with the adornment of grace. Now, whenever they go to Confession, the girls wear the necklace as a visible reminder of that miraculous transformation happening in their souls. I imagine these girls echoing the words of the prophet:

> I will greatly rejoice in the LORD,
>   my soul shall exult in my God;
> for he has clothed me with the garments of
>   salvation,
>   he has covered me with the robe of righteousness,
> as a bridegroom decks himself with a garland,
>   and as a bride adorns herself with her
>   jewels. (Isa. 61:10)

Such traditions also reflect the sacramental dimension of reality, how tangible signs can evoke spiritual realities. Because God created a marvelously interwoven world of matter and spirit and entered that world as the Word made flesh, every object and gesture can bespeak another realm. We are embodied souls meant for something beyond the material world, but we have an infinite longing and a need to express what we cannot see.

Despite these very positive associations formed by my parents, I admit that I still experienced the fear, dread, awkwardness, anticipation, shame, nervousness—add your own emotion here—that can occur even at the thought of going to Confession. I remember vividly one such moment of terror when I was about twelve or thirteen. Our Catholic grade school had the practice of going to Confession on a regular basis, but that still didn't make it easy. When it was our class's turn, we were seated in alphabetical order, which meant I should have gone first, but I managed to cling to my pew and send classmate after classmate in ahead of me. Whether it was a particular sin that weighed on me or just the dawning consciousness of sin's ugliness, I can't remember, but I dreaded the moment of entering the confessional. When I finally did, whatever burden I had been carrying was lifted, and peace and lightness filled its place. I had encountered the gentle voice of Christ speaking through the priest and leading me back to the embrace of our loving Father. When I walked out of the confessional, the rest of the class had gone, so I was free to skip and dance and twirl out of the empty church with a sense of wild abandon.

That day I learned at a deep level that fear and shame are the effects of sin, not effects of the sacrament. Rather, joy is the effect of Confession, when the soul's craving to be forgiven and to be loved "while we are yet sinners" (see Rom. 5:8) meets God's craving to forgive us and to love us unconditionally.

Now I have the privilege of teaching middle school students and witnessing the joy that comes from their reconciliation with God. But I probably learn more from them than they from me. Anyone who has taught religion to children knows that they can be profound theologians.

A sixth-grade boy named Patrick taught me one of the greatest lessons about Confession that I have yet received. It was the feast of the Dedication of St. John Lateran and an all-school Mass day. That morning, we had heard the readings of Ezekiel's vision of a river flowing out of the temple to water the trees that serve for food and medicine (Ezek. 47:1-2, 8-9, 12); St. Paul's claim to be a wise master builder and we the temples of the Holy Spirit (1 Cor. 3:9c-11, 16-17); and Christ's driving out the money changers from the temple while referring to His body as a temple (John 2:13-22). In his homily, the priest made a valiant effort to tie together all these readings for a young audience and to connect them to the dedication of a Roman basilica whose origins date back to the early fourth century. I was not sure any students had followed the thread, but it turns out at least one had.

Later that day, I was reminding my sixth graders of the Confession opportunity they would have that week and was encouraging them to take advantage of the sacrament. As I was talking, I saw Patrick's face start to glow as light bulb after light bulb went off in his mind. His hand shot up, and he was literally bouncing in his seat, wanting to share what was happening inside him. I called on him with great anticipation, and the floor was his.

"Sister, Sister," he began, "it's like what we heard at Mass." Then the following (paraphrased) torrent of theological erudition flowed out of him: "If Christ's body is the Temple, then when He hung upon the Cross and the soldier pierced His side and blood and water flowed out, it was like that river that flowed out of the temple that we heard about in the first reading. When we go to Confession, that river flowing from Christ's side takes away our sins and gives us life just like the fish and the trees. The river is like Christ's love and grace and mercy, and we are like the trees that are alive because we're living in Him. And if we are temples of the Holy Spirit too, water can flow out of us and give life to others. And, and"—at this point he was jumping up and down—"it is like the two seas in the Holy Land. The one that receives water from a river and lets the water flow out is full of fish and full of life because it gives away what it receives, but the other one is called the Dead Sea because it doesn't share what it receives with others. If we receive mercy from God in Confession, we have to share it with others; otherwise we'll be like the Dead Sea. But if we give away mercy and forgive people, we can be like the river and also like the trees. It's like God gives us medicine in Confession, so we can give medicine to others by forgiving them if they hurt us and by letting them know that God wants to forgive them, too."

Stunned silence followed as Patrick returned to his seat.

What struck me most about Patrick's reflection was his emphasis on the communal dimension of Confession. Intellectually, perhaps, I knew that, but practically I had always treated the sacrament as something that happened to us only as individuals: we go into the confessional one by one, receive our absolution and penance, say our prayers privately, then go about our business. But Patrick helped me to see that, even though it is deeply personal, Confession is not an isolated or individualistic act. In this sacrament of Reconciliation we are united to God, but also to His mystical Body and to others. Through this reunion with God, the healing waters of grace can flow into our other broken relationships as well. We cannot be like the servant who, after having his debt of a fortune canceled by the king, throttles his fellow servant for mere pocket change (see Matt. 18:23-35). No, we must give mercy as freely as we have received it. And, like the friends who bring the paralytic to Jesus (see Matt. 9:1-8), we must bring others to this sacrament of forgiveness and joy so that the whole world may experience the loving embrace of our Father who is "rich in mercy" (Eph. 2:4).

My love and appreciation for Confession has been nourished through the years by many wonderful classes, books, and retreats on the sacraments. But, I must confess, it was my parents who planted the seed with Confession and pizza nights, and the witness of students such as Patrick who have watered it the most.

CHAPTER FIVE

Anointing of the Sick

Anointing of the Sick as spoken about in

Sacred Scripture

So they went out and preached that men should re-pent. And they cast out many demons, and anointed with oil many that were sick and healed them. —Mark 6:12-13

Is any among you sick? Let him call for the elders of the church, and let them pray over him, anointing him with oil in the name of the Lord; and the prayer of faith will save the sick man, and the Lord will raise him up; and if he has committed sins, he will be forgiven. —James 5:14-15

Catechism of the Catholic Church

"By the sacred anointing of the sick and the prayer of the priests the whole Church commends those who are ill to the suffering and glorified Lord, that he may raise them up and save them. And indeed she exhorts them to contribute to the good of the People of God by freely uniting themselves to the Passion and death of Christ" (1499).

Illness and suffering have always been among the gravest problems confronted in human life. In illness, man experiences his powerlessness, his limitations, and his finitude. Every illness can make us glimpse death (1500).

Illness can lead to anguish, self-absorption, some-times even despair and revolt against God. It can also make a person more mature, helping him discern in his life what is not essential so that he can turn toward that which is. Very often illness provokes a search for God and a return to him (1501).

Moved by so much suffering Christ not only allows himself to be touched by the sick, but he makes their miseries his own: "He took our infirmities and bore our diseases". But he did not heal all the sick. His healings were signs of the coming of the Kingdom of God. They announced a more radical healing: the victory over sin and death through his Passover. On the cross Christ took upon himself the whole weight of evil and took away the "sin of the world," of which illness is only a consequence. By his passion and death on the cross Christ has given a new meaning to suffering: it can henceforth configure us to him and unite us with his redemptive Passion (1505).

The Anointing of the Sick "is not a sacrament for those only who are at the point of death. Hence, as soon as anyone of the faithful begins to be in danger of death from sickness or old age, the fitting time for him to receive this sacrament has certainly already arrived" (1514).

Only priests (bishops and presbyters) are ministers of the Anointing of the Sick. It is the duty of pastors to instruct the faithful on the benefits of this sacrament. The faithful should encourage the sick to call for a priest to receive this sacrament. The sick should prepare themselves to receive it with good dispositions, assisted by their pastor and the whole ecclesial community, which is invited to surround the sick in a special way through their prayers and fraternal attention (1516).

—————

The Greatest Aid

Of the Sacrament of Extreme Unction

It hath also seemed good to the holy Synod, to subjoin, to the preceding doctrine on penance, the following on the sacrament of Extreme Unction [now known as Anointing of the Sick], which by the Fathers was regarded as being the completion, not only of penance, but also of the whole Christian life, which ought to be a perpetual penance. First, therefore, as regards its institution, It declares and teaches, that our most gracious Redeemer—who would have his servants at all times provided with salutary remedies against all the weapons of all their enemies—as, in the other sacraments, He prepared the greatest aids, whereby, during life, Christians may preserve themselves whole from every more grievous spiritual evil, so did He guard the close of life, by the sacrament of Extreme Unction, as with a most firm defense. For though our adversary seeks and seizes opportunities, all our life long, to be able in any way to devour our souls; yet is there no time wherein he strains more vehemently all the powers of his craft to ruin us utterly, and, if he can possibly, to make us fall even from trust in the mercy of God, than when he perceives the end of our life to be at hand.

On the Institution of the Sacrament of Extreme Unction

Now, this sacred unction of the sick was instituted by Christ our Lord, as truly and properly a sacrament of the new law, insinuated indeed in Mark, but recommended and promulgated to the faithful by James the Apostle, and brother of the Lord. Is any man, he saith, sick among you? Let him bring in the priests of the Church, and let them pray over him, anointing him with oil in the name of the Lord: and the prayer of faith shall save the sick man; and the Lord shall raise him up; and if he be in sins, they shall be forgiven him. In which words, as the Church has learned from apostolic tradition, received from hand to hand, he teaches the matter, the form, the proper minister, and the effect of this salutary sacrament. For the Church has understood the matter thereof to be oil blessed by a bishop. For the unction very aptly represents the

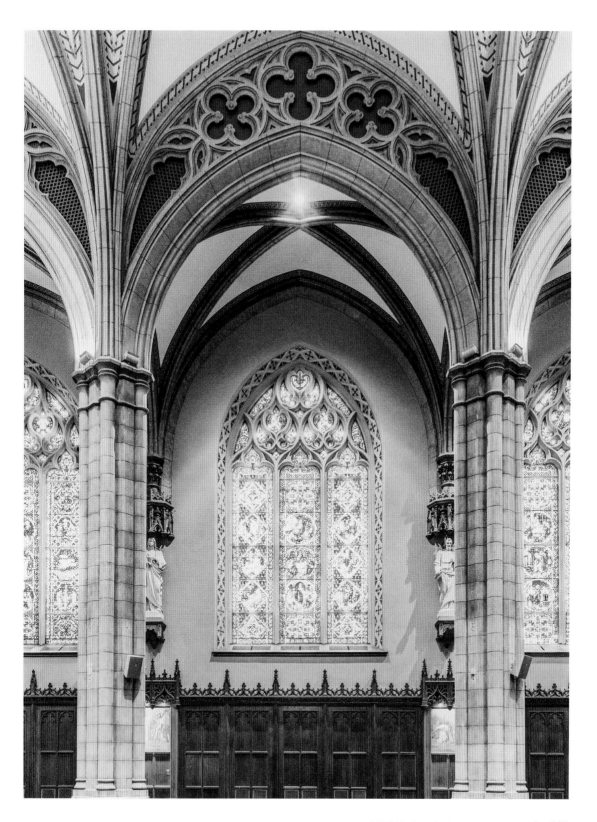

grace of the Holy Ghost with which the soul of the sick person is invisibly anointed; and furthermore that whose words, "By this unction," etc. are the form.

On the Effect of This Sacrament

Moreover the thing signified and the effect of this sacrament are explained in those words; And the prayer of faith shall save the sick man, and the Lord shall raise him up, and if he be in sins they shall be forgiven him. For the thing here signified is the grace of the Holy Ghost; whose anointing cleanses away sins, if there be any still to be expiated, as also the remains of sins; and raises up and strengthens the soul of the sick person, by exciting in him a great confidence in the divine mercy; whereby the sick being supported, bears more easily the inconveniences and pains of his sickness; and more readily resists the temptations of the devil who lies in wait for his heel; and at times obtains bodily health, when expedient for the welfare of the soul.[1]

---

1 Council of Trent, *On the Most Holy Sacraments of Penance and Extreme Unction*, session 2, chaps. 1, 2.

Anointing of the Sick Reflection by Dr. Andrew Swafford

Channel of Strength

The sacraments are the chief channels by which we receive the very life of God, the grace of the Holy Spirit. The same divine life shared within the Godhead—as the Father begets the Son, and the Holy Spirit proceeds from the embrace of the Father and the Son—this same divine life comes to us in Jesus, as He "touches" us in the sacraments, allowing "power [to] come forth" from His Mystical Body, the Church (see Luke 8:46; *CCC* 1116).

The sacraments are the means by which we enter and renew our bonds within God's covenant family. It's not an accident that *sacramentum* in Latin originally referred to an "oath"—and oaths in the ancient world formed covenant family bonds. Thus, the sacraments are the covenant oaths by which we enter into and renew our life in the family of God.

All of the sacraments are ordered to the family banquet of the most Holy Eucharist. For in all the sacraments, Christ acts by His *power*; but in the Eucharist, we have Christ *Himself*.[1] Jesus used the word "covenant" only one time—at the Last Supper; there, He fashioned the new covenant family of God through our sharing in His Body and Blood. The Church as the Bride of Christ becomes the Body of Christ through this one-flesh union in the Eucharist, this nuptial embrace, which, as Vatican II put it, is the "source and summit of Christian life."[2]

Thus, the sacraments are not simply rituals that have grown up over time—merely human customs that punctuate the ordinary course of our natural lives. Rather, the sacraments truly are salvation history made present. That is, the foundation and source of every sacrament is the Cross of Jesus Christ and the way we enter this salvation—the way we enter the story—is through the sacraments, for the sacraments make the saving Paschal Mystery, the death and Resurrection of Jesus, present for every generation.

---

1 See St. Thomas Aquinas, *Summa Theologica* III, 65, 3.
2 *LG* 11; see *CCC* 1324.

In a unique way, the sacrament of Anointing of the Sick enables us to enter into the suffering of the crucified Christ.

The Meaning of Suffering

Suffering is an inescapable and universal aspect of human existence, and great energies and resources are constantly poured into minimizing its impact.

As difficult as it is to face suffering, our faith can illumine the mystery of suffering— making it certainly not easy but perhaps more tolerable than it was before.

First, in suffering—whether it's a headache, a broken bone, or the unique spiritual and physical trials at the end of life—we come face-to-face with our finitude, our status as creatures. This is an important lesson for our technological age; it's easy for us to envisage our far-reaching scientific potential as *mastery* and *control* over the cosmos and even over the mystery of life. But in illness, in suffering, the truth becomes apparent: "In illness, man experiences his powerlessness, his

limitations, and his finitude. Every illness can make us glimpse death" (*CCC* 1500).

Further, sometimes it's only in and through suffering that one's heart is opened to hearing the voice of God. As C. S. Lewis once put it: "*God whispers* in our pleasures, but *shouts* in our pains."[3]

For my part, it was an athletic injury—a broken leg that put a dent in my college football days—that made me reevaluate where my life was going; the closing of this door was key to my entering more fully into the Catholic Faith.

In suffering, we are tested, not so God can find out whether we'll "make the team," but because athletes don't really know what they're made of until they're tested: such testing often brings something out of them that they didn't know they had.

---

3 *The Problem of Pain* (San Francisco: HarperSanFrancisco, 2001), 91, emphasis added.

When suffering has a clear purpose, such as when we suffer for the sake of our loved ones, we tend to find the resolve to get through it. But when suffering has no apparent meaning or purpose, it quickly saps our spiritual strength and vitality.

Here the Catholic teaching on "redemptive suffering" can be a salve when all seems dark. St. Paul describes it in this way: "Now I rejoice in my sufferings for your sake, and in my flesh I complete what is lacking in Christ's afflictions for the sake of his body, that is, the Church" (Col. 1:24).

What can Paul mean by our completing "what is lacking in Christ's afflictions"? Aren't Christ's sufferings on the Cross superabundant?

Christ's salvific work is indeed superabundant. But the heart of the matter (and the heart of Christianity) is for the Holy Spirit to reproduce the life, death, and Resurrection of Jesus Christ in and through each of us.

What is left to be accomplished is for us to enter into the mystery of the Cross. Nothing is lacking in Christ's suffering; but what happened to the Head must happen to His Body, the Church. That is, Christ didn't suffer so we wouldn't have to; He suffered so that our sufferings could become redemptive.

This means that our sufferings can be offered up to the Father in union with Christ and become an eminently pleasing prayer. In part, this is the meaning of the Mass: it makes the sacrifice of Christ present, so that the entire Church—Head and members—can be offered to the Father "through Him, with Him, and in Him" (see *CCC* 1368).

Further, by our sufferings in union with Jesus, *we can participate in the salvation of the world* (see *CCC* 1521). In this sense, even when we cannot see meaning in our suffering, we always know that our suffering can serve a greater purpose—we can share in the ultimate mission of saving souls. Perhaps in heaven we'll find people—maybe loved ones—who were saved precisely because of the graces we won for them when we offered up our seemingly meaningless suffering in union with our Lord.

What about Physical Healing?

Catholics don't prayerfully ask for physical healing often enough. Although it's true that Jesus "did not heal all the sick" (*CCC* 1505)—nor does He now—it is still quite possible that more might receive healing if we would implore God in faith more often. I used to be suspicious of healing ministries. But in recent years, I have been exposed to some of them in a powerful way, and I have seen the dramatic effects of this form of prayer: in one case, an elderly deaf man received his hearing right in front of me; in another, a man with a severe leg injury exhibited dramatic (but not total) improvement after having seen virtually no improvement for several months.

God does not will to heal everybody—no matter how strong our faith, no matter how ardent our prayers.

Suffering, as we noted above, can play a positive role in our salvation and the salvation of others. And even when God offers physical healing, His greater purpose is always our spiritual healing and interior conversion. Still, as children of the Father, we need not fear asking for the miracle of physical healing. Jesus told us such signs would accompany the Messianic Age (see Mark 16:17-18).

A Final Passing—Viaticum

Anybody who is seriously ill may receive Anointing of the Sick (see *CCC* 1514). Often, this sacrament accompanies a person at the end of his life. When this occurs, it is typically given in conjunction with two other sacraments: Reconciliation and the Eucharist. Reconciliation and Anointing of the Sick prepare a person for his final reception of the Most Blessed Sacrament: "As the Sacrament of Christ's Passover the Eucharist should always be the last sacrament of the earthly journey, the *viaticum* for 'passing over' to eternal life" (*CCC* 1517, emphasis added). As the eating of the Passover Lamb in the Old Testament prepared the Israelites for the Exodus, as death passed over the Israelite houses (see Exod. 12), so Jesus has brought about a New Exodus; and when we receive the new Passover Lamb in our final moments, the power of death "passes over" us as we enter eternal life. "As the sacraments of Baptism, Confirmation, and the Eucharist form a unity called 'the sacraments of Christian initiation,' so too it can be said that Penance, the Anointing of the Sick, and the Eucharist as viaticum constitute at the end of Christian life the sacraments that prepare for our heavenly homeland, the sacraments that complete the earthly pilgrimage" (*CCC* 1525).

What Does Anointing of the Sick Do?

There are two effects or consequences of sin, eternal and temporal (see *CCC* 1472, 1459). The eternal consequence of sin is hell. But sin also wounds us in the process: the way in which sin wounds us refers to the temporal consequences of sin. For this reason,

we need not only to be forgiven (i.e., freed from the eternal consequences of sin) but also to be healed and transformed (i.e., freed from the temporal consequences of sin). To use an analogy: if sin and its effects are represented by nails in a piece of wood, then the removal of the nails represents forgiveness, or the removal of the eternal consequences of sin; but even after the nails are removed, holes are left in the wood; these holes represent the temporal consequence of sin. Acts of penance, purgatory, and even indulgences have nothing to do with the eternal consequence of sin, but only the temporal: that is, they deal with the vestigial effects of sin that remain after we have been forgiven (see *CCC* 1471). Metaphorically, penance, purgatory, and indulgences help to fill in the holes in the wood after the nails have been removed (i.e., after the sin has been forgiven).

Baptism addresses both of these aspects of sin, the temporal and eternal. That is, Baptism forgives sin and all its effects (see *CCC* 1263). The sacrament of Reconciliation deals with sins committed after

Baptism (see *CCC* 1426), yet it "does not remedy all the disorders sin has caused" (*CCC* 1459); that is, the temporal consequences of sin remain after absolution (and that, in part, is why a penance is given after absolution).

In addition to offering a special healing and strengthening grace, Anointing of the Sick is also connected with the forgiveness of sins, as St. James implies when he speaks of this sacrament: "Is any one among you sick? Let him call for the elders of the Church, and let them pray over him, *anointing him with oil* in the name of the Lord; and the prayer of faith will save the sick man … if he has committed sins, *he will be forgiven*" (James 5:14-15, emphasis added; see *CCC* 1520, 1532).

Anointing of the Sick also heals the temporal wounds of sin, as Baptism does.[4] Thus, as Baptism brings about forgiveness of sin and healing of sin's temporal effects at the beginning of life, Anointing of the Sick offers this unique and total grace at the end.

Building a Culture of Life

St. John Paul II was well known for speaking of the "culture of death," by which he meant a host of contemporary ills, such as abortion and euthanasia.

John Paul II understood the culture of death as a war of the powerful against the weak—since the most vulnerable (the unborn, the elderly, and the handicapped) are most at risk—and as *tending to view suffering as the greatest of all evils*.[5]

In light of our faith, this is just not true. Of course, we should do what we can to heal and alleviate suffering. But far greater than the evil of physical suffering is the moral evil of sin. Even the great Socrates—who died about four hundred years before the coming of

---

4 See Council of Trent, sess. 14, chap. 2.

5 See *Evangelium Vitae* 12, 15.

Christ—pointed to this great truth. As he went to his death, he described two metaphorical runners—one that has caught the crowd that has just condemned him to death, and the other that is about to catch him. The faster of the two runners (i.e., wickeness) has caught the crowd, while Socrates has been caught by the slower (i.e., death). Even the pagan Socrates knew that natural death wounds the *body*, whereas committing moral evil wounds the *soul*—making the latter a far greater tragedy. Therefore, in the light of faith (and sound philosophy), suffering cannot be the greatest evil; that designation belongs to grave sin. Thus, ultimately, it's better to be murdered than to commit murder. And if physical suffering can be offered up in union with Christ, allowing us to participate in the redemption of the world, then physical suffering—rather than being the greatest evil—can become a singularly rich moment in our spiritual lives.

It's when we are weak—and stop relying simply upon our own strength—that we truly become strong. Then (and only then) do we truly allow the divine life to flow through us in an unfettered way. In those moments, His power is "made perfect in weakness" (2 Cor. 12:9). This is what the Christian life is all about—that Christ may "increase" and we may "decrease" (see John 3:30); for "it is no longer I who live, but Christ who lives in me" (Gal. 2:20).

May we always look at suffering and death from the vantage point of eternity; *for this life is not the end.*

———

Depth, Beauty, and Grace

Despite the images of solemn priests giving the Last Rites to faithful souls on their deathbeds, surrounded by mournful family and friends, the sacrament of the Anointing of the Sick offers much more depth, beauty, and grace than that caricature portrays. It may seem pointless to read a reflection on the Anointing of the Sick by a person who has never received this sacrament. But in some way, it makes perfect sense, because just as the suffering, death, and Resurrection of Christ bought each of us undeserving sinners salvation and eternal life, it is through the graces of this sacrament and the suffering and death of our brothers and sisters that each of us is drawn close to the pierced side and the Sacred Heart of Jesus. There, we are washed in His love, grace, and mercy, even, and especially, in the dark valley and at the hour of death. Every moment of life is preparation for eternal life, and every encounter with suffering is an opportunity to choose more intimacy with our Savior. As St. Ignatius of Loyola said, "If God gives you an abundant harvest of trials, it is a sign of great holiness which He desires you to attain." The fuller, more complete purpose of the Anointing of the Sick is for God to bestow on His faithful grace and strength for their journeys through the sufferings of this life into the eternity of the next. I have observed this lesson intimately in distinct experiences of suffering among my loved ones, from newborn to nearly a hundred years old.

New Life, New Suffering

When I was ten, I first witnessed the grace, beauty, and power of the Anointing of the Sick without even being present for it. After at least five years of praying every night for God to give our family another baby, my brother was born. A mere three weeks later, I was confused, terrified, and angry when a family trip was cut short by a frantic drive halfway across the country in a terrifying whirl of medical uncertainty.

As my sister and I returned home with our grandmother, my parents took our baby brother to the hospital to wait for answers. They watched their son

lie restlessly in a cold hospital crib, wires and tubes for an assortment of monitors attached to his tiny body, a cast nearly as large as his torso wrapped around his arm to keep IVs in place. The ultimate diagnosis was a serious stomach condition that required emergency surgery.

In God's divine providence, the priest at the hospital that day would many years later become a beloved pastor at our parish. But right now, he was the vessel of grace for my parents and brother as he administered the Anointing of the Sick. The grace of the sacrament in that moment was very much oriented toward giving my brother strength for treatment, surgery, and ultimately, healing. Afterward, my parents relayed how the priest anointed so gently the tiny body of my baby brother with the same sacred oils housed in our own church and offered fervent, loving prayer to God the Father on behalf of this little child. I saw then the peace that the sacrament offered my worried, grieving parents: peace to listen to wise counsel; courage to entrust their baby to a surgeon; confidence that God loves their son more than they do; peace and courage to face his divine will, knowing they had done all they could, not just as medical advocates, but also as spiritual trustees of this uniquely special life.

My parents' absolute insistence that my brother be anointed before surgery laid the foundation in my life to see suffering as spiritual. It impressed upon me that we should not attempt to suffer alone. It taught me in a real, tangible way that we truly are body *and* soul, perfectly united, and therefore, one cannot suffer or heal in the body without involving the soul, and vice versa.

Our Earthly Journey

For many of us, God willing, the sacrament of the Anointing of the Sick will be the final sacrament (that is, an outward sign of an inward grace) we receive in our earthly life, where the supernatural is made present here in the natural world. It is the bridge between our exit from this world and our entrance into the next. As such, this powerful sacrament brings beauty, joy, sustenance, and grace to souls preparing for their final journey.

Of course, today, in Holy Mother Church's wisdom and beauty, the graces of this powerful sacrament are available to the faithful earlier and more readily than ever before. This is partly a recognition that, in fact, every moment of our earthly lives is a step on our journey toward our eternal resting place, particularly when we suffer and as we near the end of our earthly lives. In those times, we are often tempted to be overwhelmed with fear and confusion. It is a battle to hang with Christ on the Cross. It is a battle to offer up our suffering for the redemption and salvation of others. It is a battle to face our mortality and the reality of eternity. We gain our strength for those battles, however long or short, simple or difficult they

may be, through the powerful sanctifying grace of the sacrament of the Anointing of the Sick.

Supernatural Grace

Many of the greatest saints not only embraced suffering as a means to holiness and intimacy with God but actually asked God to bless them with opportunities to suffer as a means of attaining grace. St. Gemma Galgani wrote, "If you really want to love Jesus, first learn to suffer, because suffering teaches you to love." Suffering is the great furnace of holiness, for it empties us of our strength and purges us of our pride, offering us the opportunity to focus completely on what is most important—the eternal.

Such dying to self requires abundant grace, and that is where the Anointing of the Sick comes into the picture. To think that we can endure alone the suffering of physical, emotional, psychological, or spiritual sickness and pain defeats its redemptive purpose. No, we must turn to God, relying on His mercy and strength. We must make a choice to unite not just our sufferings but also our wills to Christ's. These are supernatural feats that require supernatural grace, grace that is available in abundance through the sacraments of the Church and, in these particular moments, through the Sacrament of the Anointing of the Sick.

A Summer of Suffering

The summer of 2018 plunged me deep into suffering in a way that made me completely dependent for strength upon the sacraments. Within a matter of weeks, three family members received overwhelming medical diagnoses without warning. Each of them, despite vastly different diagnostic outlooks and outcomes, was fortified by the powerful sacramental graces poured out to souls in the Anointing of the Sick. My young, newlywed, newly pregnant sister was diagnosed with melanoma. My dear aunt languished inexplicably in a hospital for weeks before receiving the rare fatal diagnosis of Creutzfeldt-Jakob disease. My beloved, healthy, active father was crippled by incurable, but treatable, multiple myeloma. The darkness of that intense season of sorrow was lit only by the candle of our Faith—made real and present in our strong family bonds, supportive parish community, and life-giving sacraments administered by good, holy priests.

My sister received both a blessing for her unborn child, as well as Anointing of the Sick before her successful surgery to remove the melanoma. Through the confusion of my aunt's surprising diagnosis, she was anointed by our parish priest, who ultimately gave both her and her family the beautiful gift of a private Mass for the dying around her hospice bed only days before she died. Through months of chemo and an intense bone marrow transplant, my dad was fortified by monthly reception of the Anointing of the Sick; his treatment and recovery were remarkably without complication as he explicitly offered his nearly constant suffering for a specific personal intention.

Abundant Grace

I have learned in tangible and profound ways that grace abounds at the bedside of the sick and the dying. It is grace that heals wounds, restores brokenness, bridges divides, softens hearts, opens ears, refreshes weary souls, encourages sinners, strengthens faith, kindles love, and allows miracles. Sometimes, the miracles are physical, but more often, they are spiritual, emotional, or psychological. And much more often than we pray for or expect, the miracles are granted not to the suffering or the dying but to the ones nearby most in need of a miracle.

All of us who are blessed to walk with someone—a relative, a friend, a patient, even a stranger—through the valley of the shadow of death are fortified by the abundant and miraculous graces that Jesus' Sacred Heart pours out on those who suffer with Him. And those graces ripple through each of our lives in a thousand ways, large and small, to the greater glory of God and His kingdom. How very blessed we are!

The beauty of the Sacrament of the Anointing of the Sick has nothing to do with the outcome of the various health battles that my dear loved ones have faced. The beauty is in the strength, grace, and fortitude they received to take up their crosses and carry them, following Christ to Calvary, whether that means death for my aunt, cure for my sister, or remission for my dad. Only when we walk by choice, in faith, with the Savior can suffering be a source of great joy.

HOLY ORDERS

MARRIAGE

The Sacraments at the Service of Communion

Baptism, Confirmation, and Eucharist are sacraments of Christian initiation. They ground the common vocation of all Christ's disciples, a vocation to holiness and to the mission of evangelizing the world. They confer the graces needed for the life according to the Spirit during this life as pilgrims on the march towards the homeland.

Two other sacraments, Holy Orders and Matrimony, are directed towards the salvation of others; if they contribute as well to personal salvation, it is through service to others that they do so. They confer a particular mission in the Church and serve to build up the People of God.

Through these sacraments those already consecrated by Baptism and Confirmation for the common priesthood of all the faithful can receive particular consecrations. Those who receive the sacrament of Holy Orders are consecrated in Christ's name "to feed the Church by the word and grace of God." On their part, "Christian spouses are fortified and, as it were, consecrated for the duties and dignity of their state by a special sacrament." (CCC 1522-1535)

CHAPTER SIX

Holy Orders

Holy Orders as spoken about in

—

Sacred Scripture

"He who hears you hears me, and he who rejects you rejects me, and he who rejects me rejects him who sent me." —Luke 10:16

Let the elders who rule well be considered worthy of double honor, especially those who labor in preaching and teaching. —1 Timothy 5:17

And he took bread, and when he had given thanks he broke it and gave it to them, saying, "This is my body which is given for you. Do this in remembrance of me." —Luke 22:19

———

Catechism of the Catholic Church

Holy Orders is the sacrament through which the mission entrusted by Christ to his apostles continues to be exercised in the Church until the end of time: thus it is the sacrament of apostolic ministry. It includes three degrees: episcopate, presbyterate, and diaconate (1536).

Christ, high priest and unique mediator, has made of the Church "a kingdom, priests for his God and Father." The whole community of believers is, as such, priestly. The faithful exercise their baptismal priesthood through their participation, each according to his own vocation, in Christ's mission as priest, prophet, and king. Through the sacraments of Baptism and Confirmation the faithful are "consecrated to be . . . a holy priesthood (1546).

The ministerial or hierarchical priesthood of bishops and priests, and the common priesthood of all the faithful participate, "each in its own proper way, in the one priesthood of Christ." While being "ordered one to another," they differ essentially. In what sense?

While the common priesthood of the faithful is exercised by the unfolding of baptismal grace—a life of faith, hope, and charity, a life according to the Spirit—the ministerial priesthood is at the service of the common priesthood. It is directed at the unfolding of the baptismal grace of all Christians. The ministerial priesthood is a *means* by which Christ unceasingly builds up and leads his Church. For this reason it is transmitted by its own sacrament, the sacrament of Holy Orders (1547).

In the ecclesial service of the ordained minister, it is Christ himself who is present to his Church as Head of his Body, Shepherd of his flock, high priest of the redemptive sacrifice, Teacher of Truth. This is what the Church means by saying that the priest, by virtue of the sacrament of Holy Orders, acts *in persona Christi Capitis*:

> It is the same priest, Christ Jesus, whose sacred person his minister truly represents. Now the minister, by reason of the sacerdotal consecration

which he has received, is truly made like to the high priest and possesses the authority to act in the power and place of the person of Christ himself *(virtute ac persona ipsius Christi).*

Christ is the source of all priesthood: the priest of the old law was a figure of Christ, and the priest of the new law acts in the person of Christ (1548).

The ministerial priesthood has the task not only of representing Christ—Head of the Church—before the assembly of the faithful, but also of acting in the name of the whole Church when presenting to God the prayer of the Church, and above all when offering the Eucharistic sacrifice (1552).

"The divinely instituted ecclesiastical ministry is exercised in different degrees by those who even from ancient times have been called bishops, priests, and deacons." Catholic doctrine, expressed in the liturgy, the Magisterium, and the constant practice of the Church, recognizes that there are two degrees of

ministerial participation in the priesthood of Christ: the episcopacy and the presbyterate. The diaconate is intended to help and serve them. For this reason the term *sacerdos* in current usage denotes bishops and priests but not deacons. Yet Catholic doctrine teaches that the degrees of priestly participation (episcopate and presbyterate) and the degree of service (diaconate) are all three conferred by a sacramental act called "ordination," that is, by the sacrament of Holy Orders:

> Let everyone revere the deacons as Jesus Christ, the bishop as the image of the Father, and the presbyters as the senate of God and the assembly of the apostles. For without them one cannot speak of the Church (1554).

"Amongst those various offices which have been exercised in the Church from the earliest times the chief place, according to the witness of tradition, is held by the function of those who, through their appointment to the dignity and responsibility of bishop, and in virtue consequently of the unbroken succession going back to the beginning, are regarded as transmitters of the apostolic line" (1555).

To fulfill their exalted mission, "the apostles were endowed by Christ with a special outpouring of the Holy Spirit coming upon them, and by the imposition of hands they passed on to their auxiliaries the gift of the Spirit, which is transmitted down to our day through episcopal consecration" (1556).

Through the sacrament of Holy Orders priests share in the universal dimensions of the mission that Christ entrusted to the apostles. The spiritual gift they have received in ordination prepares them, not for a limited and restricted mission, "but for the fullest, in fact the universal mission of salvation 'to the end of the earth,'" "prepared in spirit to preach the Gospel everywhere" (1565).

"It is in the Eucharistic cult or in the *Eucharistic assembly* of the faithful *(synaxis)* that they exercise in a supreme degree their sacred office; there, acting in the person of Christ and proclaiming his mystery, they unite the votive offerings of the faithful to the sacrifice of Christ their head, and in the sacrifice of the Mass they make present again and apply, until the coming of the Lord, the unique sacrifice of the New Testament, that namely of Christ offering himself once for all a spotless victim to the Father." From this unique sacrifice their whole priestly ministry draws its strength (1566).

"The priests, prudent cooperators of the episcopal college and its support and instrument, called to the service of the People of God, constitute, together with their bishop, a unique sacerdotal college *(presbyterium)* dedicated, it is, true to a variety of distinct duties. In each local assembly of the faithful they represent, in a certain sense, the bishop, with whom they are associated in all trust and generosity; in part they take upon themselves his duties and solicitude and in their daily toils discharge them." Priests can exercise their ministry only in dependence on the bishop and in communion with him. The promise of obedience they make to the bishop at the moment of ordination and the kiss of peace from him at the end of the ordination liturgy mean that the bishop considers them his co-workers, his sons, his brothers and his friends, and that they in return owe him love and obedience (1567).

"All priests, who are constituted in the order of priesthood by the sacrament of Order, are bound together by an intimate sacramental brotherhood, but in a special way they form one priestly body in the diocese to which they are attached under their own bishop. . . ." The unity of the presbyterium finds liturgical expression in the custom of the presbyters' imposing hands, after the bishop, during the Ate of ordination (1568).

Deacons share in Christ's mission and grace in a special way. The sacrament of Holy Orders marks them with an *imprint* ("character") which cannot be removed and which configures them to Christ, who made himself the "deacon" or servant of all. Among other tasks, it is the task of deacons to assist the bishop and priests in the celebration of the divine mysteries, above all the Eucharist, in the distribution of Holy Communion, in assisting at and blessing marriages, in the proclamation of the Gospel and preaching, in presiding over funerals, and in dedicating themselves to the various ministries of charity (1570).

The Priest

For the priestly office is indeed discharged on earth, but it ranks among heavenly ordinances; and very naturally so: for neither man, nor angel, nor archangel, nor any other created power, but the Paraclete Himself, instituted this vocation, and persuaded men while still abiding in the flesh to represent the ministry of angels. Wherefore the consecrated priest ought to be as pure as if he were standing in the heavens themselves in the midst of those powers. Fearful, indeed, and of most awful import, were the things which were used before the dispensation of grace, as the bells, the pomegranates, the stones on the breastplate and on the ephod, the girdle, the mitre, the long robe, the plate of gold, the holy of holies, the deep silence within. But if any one should examine the things which belong to the dispensation of grace, he will find that, small as they are, yet are they fearful and full of awe, and that what was spoken concerning the law is true in this case also, that *what has been made glorious has no glory in this respect by reason of the glory which excels* (2 Cor. 3:10). For when you see the Lord sacrificed, and laid upon the altar, and

the priest standing and praying over the victim, and all the worshippers empurpled with that precious blood, can you then think that you are still among men, and standing upon the earth? Are you not, on the contrary, straightway translated to Heaven, and casting out every carnal thought from the soul, do you not with disembodied spirit and pure reason contemplate the things which are in Heaven? Oh! What a marvel! What love of God to man! He who sits on high with the Father is at that hour held in the hands of all, and gives Himself to those who are willing to embrace and grasp Him. And this all do through the eyes of faith! Do these things seem to you fit to be despised, or such as to make it possible for anyone to be uplifted against them?

Would you also learn from another miracle the exceeding sanctity of this office? Picture Elijah and the vast multitude standing around him, and the sacrifice laid upon the altar of stones, and all the rest of the people hushed into a deep silence while the prophet alone offers up prayer: then the sudden

rush of fire from Heaven upon the sacrifice:— these are marvelous things, charged with terror. Now then pass from this scene to the rites which are celebrated in the present day; they are not only marvelous to behold, but transcendent in terror. There stands the priest, not bringing down fire from Heaven, but the Holy Spirit: and he makes prolonged supplication, not that some flame sent down from on high may consume the offerings, but that grace descending on the sacrifice may thereby enlighten the souls of all, and render them more refulgent than silver purified by fire. Who can despise this most awful mystery, unless he is stark mad and senseless? Or do you not know that no human soul could have endured that fire in the sacrifice, but all would have been utterly consumed, had not the assistance of God's grace been great.

For if any one will consider how great a thing it is for one, being a man, and compassed with flesh and blood, to be enabled to draw near to that blessed and pure nature, he will then clearly see what great honor the grace of the Spirit has vouchsafed to priests; since by their agency these rites are celebrated, and others nowise inferior to these both in respect of our dignity and our salvation. For they who inhabit the earth and make their abode there are entrusted with the administration of things which are in Heaven, and have received an authority which God has not given to angels or archangels. For it has not been said to them, *Whatsoever you shall bind on earth shall be bound in Heaven, and whatsoever you shall loose on earth shall be loosed in Heaven* (Matt. 18:18). They who rule on earth have indeed authority to bind, but only the body: whereas this binding lays hold of the soul and penetrates the heavens; and what priests do here below God ratifies above, and the Master confirms the sentence of his servants. For indeed what is it but all manner of heavenly authority which He has given them when He says, Whose sins ye remit they are remitted, and *whose sins ye retain they are retained* (John 20:23)? What authority could be greater than this? *The Father has committed all judgment to the Son* (John 5:22)? But I see it all put into the hands of these men by the Son. For they have been conducted to this dignity as if they were already translated to Heaven, and had transcended human nature, and were released from the passions to which we are liable. Moreover, if a king should bestow this honor upon any of his subjects, authorizing him to cast into prison whom he pleased and to release them again, he becomes an object of envy and respect to all men; but he who has received from God an authority as much greater as heaven is more precious than earth, and souls more precious than bodies, seems to some to have received so small an honor that they are actually able to imagine that one of those who have been entrusted with these things will despise the gift. Away with such madness! For transparent madness it is to despise so great a dignity, without which it is not possible to obtain either our own salvation, or the good things which have been promised to us. For if no one can enter into the kingdom of Heaven except he be regenerate through water and the Spirit, and he who does not eat the flesh of the Lord and drink His blood is excluded from eternal life, and if all these things are accomplished only by means of those holy hands, I mean the hands of the priest, how will any one, without these, be able to escape the fire of hell, or to win those crowns which are reserved for the victorious?[1]

---

1 John Chrysostom, *On the Priesthood*, bk. 3, pars. 4, 5.

The Daily Battle

We had scraped up enough money to get her a round-trip ticket to New Jersey so that she could see her children. We figured she would not make the return trip. My friend Maureen was dying of cancer, and I was newly ordained. Her cancer quickly overtook her, and she could not leave her daughter's house. I asked permission of my pastor to visit her and to give her the sacraments, and he agreed. I packed a Mass kit and boarded a plane. No one on the plane knew of the rescue mission that God was orchestrating, but there were souls in the balance, and He was going to use one of his priests. I couldn't believe he chose me. The hospital table became a little altar, much like the one we had made as kids, but this time, there was no make-believe. There in her room, after being anointed, Maureen received Holy Communion. She had offered her sufferings for the reconciliation of her children, many of whom had left the Church. Each was reconciled privately during that visit, and Maureen's face streamed with tears as God answered her deepest desire. She watched each of her children receive Holy Communion and then died a few hours later with a peaceful smile. It was the feast of Our Lady of Lourdes, February 11, 2001.

The death of Maureen was a marked moment in my early priesthood. I was quickly becoming more and more aware of the battle between the principalities. In seminary, we had studied the four last things—Death, Judgment, Heaven, and Hell—but the reality of this daily battle for souls was now becoming the reason to wake and to rise for prayer each day. Just a little more than seven months before Maureen's death, I had received the humbling and beautiful sacrament of Holy Orders. Exactly seven months after Maureen's death, on September 11, 2001, the entire world would see clearly the reality of evil in our midst. As I watched this horror and the devastating loss of life unfold before me, strangely, I was not frightened. I reached for my Mass kit and set up the altar. This great and terrible suffering had to be united with Christ's eternal sacrifice and offered by the simple hands of a priest.

Early Seeds

A vocation to the priesthood emerges not in isolation but from the family, the parish, and the holy examples of parents, priests, and religious. This was certainly the case in my life. My earliest memories of the priesthood came from Fr. Thomas Williams. He was present to my parents—young parents with seven children—and he would visit them, pray with them, and listen to them. I believe he brought them much comfort. Each day, after we had dropped off my brothers and sisters at their schools, I would accompany Mom to daily Mass. This was a quite a treat for me. Often, we were the only ones at morning Mass. Like clockwork, Fr. Williams would appear at the side door of the sacristy. He would open the door, ring the mounted bell, and appear in vestments with his veiled chalice. On August 17, 1967, Fr. Williams did not come through that door because, as we learned later, he had died in the night. It was a sad day, and I remember asking myself, "Who will offer the sacrifice of the Mass? Who will raise the chalice?" Little did

I know, at such a young age, that these questions would become the seeds of my vocation in pretty spectacular ways.

Avoiding the Call

Throughout high school and college, I attended Mass faithfully, but no one asked me about my discernment, and so, with success in school and business, I had ample means to plan my life and to avoid tending to those early seeds of my vocation. Msgr. Ronald Knox once said, "It is a futile effort to hide oneself from the Divine pursuit." And yet we do this for a big part of our lives. We become captured by the vanity that comes from our accomplishments and from the enticement of the next goal. Priesthood can never be realized as a goal or a personal pursuit; it is a divine pursuit. Only when a man dies to his desires, allowing God to animate him, can his true calling in life begin. This is because the priesthood finds it heart in sacrifice, a willingness to lay down one's life in love for the other. This becomes vividly clear in the *Rite of Ordination* when a young man lies down on the marble, like a dead man, waiting for the Holy Spirit to quicken him to new life.

Confrontation with Mortality

At age thirty in the summer of 1992, I was living in Chicago, accomplishing great things in my professional life. My parents, now retired, were on their first vacation. Relaxing after a day of golf on Edisto Island, hours away from the closest hospital, my father had a debilitating stroke. Mom and Dad were heroes to my siblings and me. Their faith was such a deep part of their marriage, and they seemed invincible because of that faith. The sudden shock of seeing this hero of mine, paralyzed on the left side and humbled to the point of needing help with basic tasks such as eating, personal hygiene, and dressing himself affected me deeply, and it frightened me. It made me ask myself whether the path I was following was the right path, or could it be that I was following my own path? I returned home, and my parish priest, who had given me first Holy Communion, asked me if I had ever thought about the priesthood. I said yes, and he gave me the vocation director's card. I will always be grateful to Fr. John Harper. He was brave enough to ask and to encourage me to discern God's will. I believe God used my father's stroke to wake me up. Before I knew it, I had entered formal discernment and was accepted into seminary. Six years later, God had radically changed my course, and I was called to Holy Orders by my bishop.

Ordination and Miracles

I could go on about the glorious day and humbling experience of having the grace of the Holy Spirit called down upon me by the hands of my bishop, or the incredible experience of being at the altar for the first time. One of the most touching parts of the day was giving my parents Holy Communion. They had nourished me all my life, and now, in a deeply mysterious way, God was using me, an imperfect

creature to communicate Himself, the Real Presence, to my dear parents.

In the first week of my priesthood, there were times when I wondered if something might be wrong. I was assigned to a very large parish, and I had celebrated Holy Mass, Baptism, and Marriage, but no one had asked me to hear his confession. I loved the Sacrament of Confession; it had been such an important part of my life, and I longed to give absolution. Instead, I felt like half a priest. That first week, I had to return to Washington to pick up my books and my boxes from seminary. It was a hot day in July, and I was wearing not clerics but shorts, an orange T-shirt, and flip flops. I stopped to get coffee for the long drive home, and there on my left was a homeless man passed out in the bushes. I leaned over to check on him and asked if he was okay. He sat up, opened his eyes, and said, "I'm a Catholic, and I want to go to Confession." I couldn't believe it! There was nothing about my clothes that indicated that I was a priest, so I said to him, "I'm a priest." I believe God waited for me to show faith before He confirmed His gift with the first of many consolations.

After that trip to Washington, I returned to my parish and stopped in to visit the other associate pastor, my friend, Fr. Bill. As we relaxed in his office and discussed the whirlwind of the first week, I look up at his bookcase. I was completely stunned. I saw a chalice, and I said, "I know that chalice." I asked him where he acquired it. Fr. Bill said that it was given to him out of the archives. I asked him to take it down and turn it over and read to me the name on it. My heart sung as he said, "Father Thomas Williams." I asked him if I could borrow it next month on August 17, and he asked why. I replied that this was his date of death, that I had been a little five-year-old the day he didn't ring the bell and go to the altar, and that I would like to raise his chalice and say a Mass for the repose of his soul. Those original questions, "Who will offer the sacrifice of the Mass? And who will raise the chalice?" were the seeds of my vocation. With tender care from my parents, the priests, and the religious in my life, those seeds of God's divine pursuit had blossomed thirty-three years later.

Recently, I was diagnosed with terminal cancer. Although it was frightening to learn of it, a deep sense of peace resounds in my heart. I have been awed by the consolations that God has given through the prayers of so many. On a recent trip to a conference, a holy cardinal prayed for me to bear it with grace and asked that the cancer be offered for the purification of the Church. This mission has given me something new to offer each day, and it is a reminder that God is in charge. He doesn't want part of us; He wants all of us. And so it is my hope and prayer that God will plant those seeds in the hearts of a new generation, who will ask those simple questions: "Who will offer the sacrifice of the Mass? Who will raise the chalice?" He will answer in spectacular ways.

CHAPTER SEVEN

Marriage

Marriage as spoken about in

Sacred Scripture

And Pharisees came up and in order to test him asked, "Is it lawful for a man to divorce his wife?" He answered them, "What did Moses command you?" They said, "Moses allowed a man to write a certificate of divorce, and to put her away." But Jesus said to them, "For your hardness of heart he wrote you this commandment. But from the beginning of creation, 'God made them male and female.' 'For this reason a man shall leave his father and mother and be joined to his wife, and the two shall become one.' So they are no longer two but one. What therefore God has joined together, let not man put asunder." —Mark 10:2-9

Marriage according to the

———

Catechism of the Catholic Church

"The matrimonial covenant, by which a man and a woman establish between themselves a partnership of the whole of life, is by its nature ordered toward the good of the spouses and the procreation and education of offspring; this covenant between baptized persons has been raised by Christ the Lord to the dignity of a sacrament (1601).

Sacred Scripture begins with the creation of man and woman in the image and likeness of God and concludes with a vision of "the wedding-feast of the Lamb." Scripture speaks throughout of marriage and its "mystery," its institution and the meaning God has given it, its origin and its end, its various realizations throughout the history of salvation, the difficulties arising from sin and its renewal "in the Lord" in the New Covenant of Christ and the Church (1602).

God who created man out of love also calls him to love the fundamental and innate vocation of every human being. For man is created in the image and likeness of God who is himself love. Since God created him man and woman, their mutual love becomes an image of the absolute and unfailing love with which God loves man. It is good, very good, in the Creator's eyes. And this love which God blesses is intended to be fruitful and to be realized in the common work of watching over creation: "And God blessed them, and God said to them: 'Be fruitful and multiply, and fill the earth and subdue it' "(1604).

Holy Scripture affirms that man and woman were created for one another: "It is not good that the man should be alone." The woman, "flesh of his flesh," his equal, his nearest in all things, is given to him by God as a "helpmate"; she thus represents God from whom comes our help. "Therefore a man leaves his father and his mother and cleaves to his wife, and they become one flesh." The Lord himself shows that this signifies an unbreakable union of their two lives

by recalling what the plan of the Creator had been "in the beginning": "So they are no longer two, but one flesh" (1605).

The entire Christian life bears the mark of the spousal love of Christ and the Church. Already Baptism, the entry into the People of God, is a nuptial mystery; it is so to speak the nuptial bath which precedes the wedding feast, the Eucharist. Christian marriage in its turn becomes an efficacious sign, the sacrament of the covenant of Christ and the Church. Since it signifies and communicates grace, marriage between baptized persons is a true sacrament of the New Covenant (1617).

———

The Union

The true origin of marriage, venerable brothers, is well known to all. Though revilers of the Christian faith refuse to acknowledge the never-interrupted doctrine of the Church on this subject, and have long striven to destroy the testimony of all nations and of all times, they have nevertheless failed not only to quench the powerful light of truth, but even to lessen it. We record what is to all known, and cannot be doubted by any, that God, on the sixth day of creation, having made man from the slime of the earth, and having breathed into his face the breath of life, gave him a companion, whom He miraculously took from the side of Adam when he was locked in sleep. God thus, in His most far-reaching foresight, decreed that this husband and wife should be the natural beginning of the human race, from whom it might be propagated and preserved by an unfailing fruitfulness throughout all futurity of time. And this union of man and woman, that it might answer more fittingly to the infinite wise counsels of God, even from the beginning manifested chiefly two most excellent properties—deeply sealed, as it were, and

signed upon it—namely, unity and perpetuity. From the Gospel we see clearly that this doctrine was declared and openly confirmed by the divine authority of Jesus Christ. He bore witness to the Jews and to His Apostles that marriage, from its institution, should exist between two only, that is, between one man and one woman; that of two they are made, so to say, one flesh; and that the marriage bond is by the will of God so closely and strongly made fast that no man may dissolve it or render it asunder. "For this cause shall a man leave father and mother, and shall cleave to his wife, and they two shall be in one flesh. Therefore now they are not two, but one flesh. What, therefore, God hath joined together, let no man put asunder."

This form of marriage, however, so excellent and so pre-eminent, began to be corrupted by degrees, and to disappear among the heathen; and became even among the Jewish race clouded in a measure and obscured. For in their midst a common custom was gradually introduced, by which it was accounted as lawful for a man to have more than one wife; and

eventually when "by reason of the hardness of their heart," Moses indulgently permitted them to put away their wives, the way was open to divorce.

But what was decreed and constituted in respect to marriage by the authority of God has been more fully and more clearly handed down to us, by tradition and the written Word, through the Apostles, those heralds of the laws of God. To the Apostles, indeed, as our masters, are to be referred the doctrines which "our holy Fathers, the Councils, and the Tradition of the Universal Church have always taught," namely, that Christ our Lord raised marriage to the dignity of a sacrament; that to husband and wife, guarded and strengthened by the heavenly grace which His merits gained for them, He gave power to attain holiness in the married state; and that, in a wondrous way, making marriage an example of the mystical union between Himself and His Church, He not only perfected that love which is according to nature, but also made the naturally indivisible union of one man with one woman far more perfect through the bond of heavenly love. Paul says to the Ephesians: "Husbands, love your wives, as Christ also loved the Church, and delivered Himself up for it, that He might sanctify it. . . . So also ought men to love their wives as their own bodies. . . . For no man ever hated his own flesh, but nourisheth and cherisheth it, as also Christ doth the Church; because we are members of His body, of His flesh, and of His bones. For this cause shall a man leave his father and mother, and shall cleave to his wife, and they shall be two in one flesh. This is a great sacrament; but I speak in Christ and in the Church." In like manner from the teaching of the Apostles we learn that the unity of marriage and its perpetual indissolubility, the indispensable conditions of its very origin, must, according to the command of Christ, be holy and inviolable without exception. Paul says again: "To them that are married, not I, but the Lord commandeth that the wife depart not from her husband; and if she depart, that she remain unmarried or be reconciled to her husband." And again: "A woman is bound by the law as long as her husband liveth; but if her husband die, she is at liberty." It is for these reasons that marriage is "a great sacrament"; "honorable in all," holy, pure, and to be reverenced as a type and symbol of most high mysteries.

Furthermore, the Christian perfection and completeness of marriage are not comprised in those points only which have been mentioned. For, first, there has been vouchsafed to the marriage union a higher and nobler purpose than was ever previously given to it. By the command of Christ, it not only looks to the propagation of the human race, but to the bringing forth of children for the Church, "fellow citizens with the saints, and the domestics of God"; so that "a people might be born and brought up for the worship and religion of the true God and our Savior Jesus Christ."

Now, since the family and human society at large spring from marriage, there are men who will on no account allow matrimony to be the subject of the jurisdiction of the Church. Nay, they endeavor to deprive it of all holiness, and so bring it within the contracted sphere of those rights which, having been instituted by man, are ruled and administered by the civil jurisprudence of the community. Wherefore it necessarily follows that they attribute all power over marriage to civil rulers, and allow none whatever to the Church; and, when the Church exercises any such power, they think that she acts either by favor of the civil authority or to its injury. Now is the time, they say, for the heads of the State to vindicate their rights unflinchingly, and to do their best to settle all that relates to marriage according as to them seems good.

Hence are owing civil marriages, commonly so called; hence laws are framed which impose impediments to marriage; hence arise judicial sentences affecting the marriage contract, as to whether or not it have been rightly made. Lastly, all power of prescribing and passing judgment in this class of cases is, as we see, of set purpose denied to the Catholic Church, so that no regard is paid either to her divine power or to her prudent laws. Yet, under these, for so many centuries, have the nations lived on whom the light of civilization shone bright with the wisdom of Christ Jesus.

Nevertheless, the naturalists, as well as all who profess that they worship above all things the divinity of the State, and strive to disturb whole communities with such wicked doctrines, cannot escape the charge of delusion. Marriage has God for its author, and was from the very beginning a kind of foreshadowing of the Incarnation of His Son; and therefore there abides in it a something holy and religious; not extraneous, but innate; not derived from men, but implanted by nature. Innocent III, therefore and Honorius III, our predecessors, affirmed not falsely nor rashly that a sacrament of marriage existed ever amongst the faithful and unbelievers. We call to witness the monuments of antiquity, as also the manners and customs of those people who, being the most civilized, had the greatest knowledge of law and equity. In the minds of all of them it was a fixed and foregone conclusion that, when marriage was thought of, it was thought of as conjoined with religion and holiness. Hence, among those, marriages were commonly celebrated with religious ceremonies, under the authority of pontiffs, and with the ministry of priests. So mighty, even in the souls ignorant of heavenly doctrine, was the force of nature, of the remembrance of their origin, and of the conscience of the human race. As, then, marriage is holy by its own power, in its own nature, and of itself, it ought not to be regulated and administered by the will of civil rulers, but by the divine authority of the Church, which alone in sacred matters professes the office of teaching.

Next, the dignity of the sacrament must be considered, for through addition of the sacrament the marriages of Christians have become far the noblest of all matrimonial unions. But to decree and ordain concerning the sacrament is, by the will of Christ Himself, so much a part of the power and duty of the Church that it is plainly absurd to maintain that even the very smallest fraction of such power has been transferred to the civil ruler.

Let special care be taken that the people be well instructed in the precepts of Christian wisdom, so that they may always remember that marriage was not

instituted by the will of man, but, from the very beginning, by the authority and command of God; that
it does not admit of plurality of wives or husbands;
that Christ, the author of the New Covenant, raised
it from a rite of nature to be a sacrament, and gave to
His Church legislative and judicial power with regard
to the bond of union. On this point the very greatest
care must be taken to instruct them, lest their minds
should be led into error by the unsound conclusions
of adversaries who desire that the Church should be
deprived of that power.[1]

---

1   Leo XIII, Encyclical on Christian Marriage *Arcanum*
    (February 10, 1880), nos. 5, 6, 9-10, 17-20, 39. (Inter-
    nal citations omitted.)

———

The Heart of Marriage

The matrimonial covenant, by which a man and a woman establish between themselves a partnership of the whole of life, is by its nature ordered toward the good of the spouses. The answer is clearly articulated by the *Catechism of the Catholic Church*:

> "The matrimonial covenant, by which a man and a woman establish between themselves a partnership of the whole of life, is by its nature ordered toward the good of the spouses and the procreation and education of offspring; this covenant between baptized persons has been raised by Christ the Lord to the dignity of a sacrament." (*CCC*, 1601)

Marriage, then, is no mystery but is well defined. And I might well continue to unpack this definition, exploring what marriage is and isn't by citing Church Fathers, Church documents, philosophers, and theologians.

But this would be talking about marriage from the outside, and it would be a mistake. I want to speak of marriage from the inside. That is, I want to speak from the heart, not about what marriage *is*, but what marriage *means*. For marriage is not merely a solemnly defined article in a catechism; it is not an abstraction or an idea for academics to toy with. Like all sacraments, it is a lived experienced, a concrete reality. And it is of this reality that I want to speak.

When I was younger, and indeed more immature, I viewed marriage as the fulfillment of my longings. It was the answer, I believed, to my hunger for intimacy, to my desire for affirmation, and yes, even to my sexual urges. If only I could find a wife, I imagined, I would be content.

Eventually, I did find a beautiful woman whom I loved, and who, wonder of wonders, loved me in return. We quickly became engaged and began preparing for marriage. I eagerly pored over marriage books and articles and listened to countless talks

about how to be a good husband. In my naivete, I was quite convinced that I knew exactly what marriage was about, and I would no doubt be a wonderful and enviable husband. I understood marriage from the outside, and not from the inside.

But then I got married. No sooner had I done so than I came face-to-face with the ugliness of my own immaturity, my own selfishness, my own pride. It was jarring and unpleasant, to say the least. Wasn't I better than this? Didn't I know more about marriage than most young husbands? How can I hurt so often the woman I love? What is wrong with me?

These questions and more plagued the early days of our marriage, for I felt like a complete failure as a husband within a very short time. Despite my real love for my wife, I endlessly chose my needs and desires over hers, and I could not understand why.

What I did not realize then, and do realize now, is that marriage is not about self-fulfillment. It is certainly not about satisfying sexual cravings or about mere emotional affirmation. It is a school of love. And as a school of love, it is a duel to the death with our disordered passions and lusts. It is a daily dying to our sinful selves. It is a moment-by-moment choosing of the way of the cross, which is the way of sacrifice.

Marriage, rightly lived, will indeed bring you more joy than you can possibly imagine. But you cannot find this joy by seeking it directly. This will only lead to disillusionment. "Whoever would save his life will lose it," our Lord tells us, "and whoever loses his life for my sake will find it" (Matt. 16:25). Life can be found only through surrendering it. So too with the joy of marriage—it can be found only through self-forgetfulness and self-gift.

My wife and I have been married for eight years, and although I know it is almost a cliché to say it, I love her more now than I did when we got married. Through our years of marriage, I have learned much about authentic love and sacrifice (though I still have much to learn). And yet I have also realized that no matter how much I give to my wife, she has given me far more.

It is not enough to know that God loves us in an abstract sense. We must experience His unconditional love and mercy in a concrete way, and we most often do so through other people. My experience of God's love has come most profoundly through my wife.

I brought many insecurities and self-doubts into our marriage. I feared fully revealing myself to anyone, lest I be despised and rejected, and as a result, I had erected many defenses to guard myself from emotional vulnerability. Some of these defenses were harmless, while others led me to wound the woman I loved.

But despite my frequent foolishness, my insecurities began to heal one by one through my wife's relentless love. Through her forgiveness and unconditional acceptance, I received a rare and precious gift—the gift of being fully loved as myself. My defenses began to drop; my heart began to heal. I learned the meaning

of true intimacy and the joy that it can bring. And I am still learning it.

Marriage is a sacrament, a channel of grace, a way to know and experience the love of God. St. Paul tells us that it is a great mystery that illustrates the relationship between Christ and His Church. Reflecting upon these truths, I see that there is one defining attribute that characterizes this mystical marriage between the Lord and His people more than any other: mercy.

Why did the Eternal Word, the brightness of the Father, humble Himself, take on flesh, and descend into Mary's womb? To save us from our sins. Why did the Lord of all creation allow Himself to be beaten, mocked, and nailed to a cross? To forgive us, to reconcile us, to demonstrate His unfathomable love for us. "One will hardly die for a righteous man," St. Paul says in breathless astonishment. "But . . . while we were yet sinners Christ died for us" (Rom. 5:7-8).

Mercy is at the heart of our redemption. And it is at the heart of marriage. Giving and receiving it. Being healed by it. I am firmly convinced that we come closest to the heart of marriage when we forgive—when we see each other exactly as we are, sins and all, and lay down our lives for one another anyway.

I began this article speaking about sacrifice and self-gift. In our self-indulgent age, these are dirty words. We associate them with pain, discomfort, even misery. Yet, for one who has experienced mercy, sacrifice is no burden. It flows naturally from the heart. It is the greatest joy.

In my marriage, I have indeed given much to my wife and children over the years. But nothing I have done can compare with what they have given me: a glimpse of the mercy and love of the Lord Jesus. Our marriages, our families, must become schools of genuine love and mercy. For if we love one another unconditionally, if we mercifully accept one another exactly as we are, we will experience a joy beyond description and a very real foretaste of heaven. Even more, our homes will become beacons radiating life and light to a world hungry for the love of God.

Above all hold unfailing your love for one another, since love covers a multitude of sins. (1 Pet. 4:8)

GRATIARUM ACTIO

PROPITIATIO

———

A Call to Love

I am not an expert on living out the Sacrament of Marriage—as I am writing this, my husband and I have been married only eight blissful weeks. What I can share, however, is the way we prepared for marriage and our hopes to live out that preparation in the years to come. Our few weeks of marriage are a fulfillment of many years of anticipation and growth and the promise of many more years of joyful labor and continual renewal of God's plans for us.

Years before I got married, a wise priest told me to take the time to "read the book of my life." I was a college student then and was on my journey into the Catholic Church. The priest, who would later give me my first sacraments, explained that we should study our own childhoods—including our parents' marriage—as adults, to look at what was good and beautiful, what was wrong or bad, and what was missing. This would help us unlock our own future.

There's no better way to honor our parents than to strive to do better than they did—standing on their shoulders. If we don't take the time for self-reflection, it is easy to hold attitudes or to make choices that are harmful, that prevent our hearts from loving well, whether in marriage or in another calling. Many of us grew up in broken homes or with poor models of marriage, if any model at all. From our parents' example, whether we realize it or not, we obtain our most powerful definition of how to be a mother, father, wife, or husband. If there's divorce or separation, that shapes our understanding of marriage. If there is conflict or abuse, it will color our view of love and marriage. Some of us have lost the beautiful vision of what marriage is designed to be; some were never given the gift of this vision at all.

Christ's Church teaches us the essential truth that love is the key to life. We are all called to live out love, whether single, married, or following a religious vocation. And since true love is the gift of one's own self, it is a high challenge, requiring our gift today and spurring us on to be better tomorrow, so that we have more to give.

Every person has a call—and we each receive that call at different times. But the call is to always trust and to grow closer to Jesus. Sometimes we don't understand circumstances or why things happen the way they do. We aren't promised the specific vocation of marriage, the priesthood, religious life—in fact, we aren't even promised tomorrow. The best thing we can do is live each day willing to begin again, and trust that our Lord will protect and guide us each step of the way.

I was born into a big, homeschooling family of eight children. We weren't raised Catholic—my parents were Protestant while we were young—but faith was very important to my parents. We went to church every Sunday and attended regular family Bible studies. There was great joy in having so many siblings and being raised with the truth that we were God's

children and that we each had a purpose in life to do good for Him. There was also the chaos that can come with a big family, and the conflicts and sometimes painful lessons of having young parents who themselves were still growing up and healing from their own childhood wounds.

It took years of prayer and patience to understand my childhood, to see the many beautiful things I knew I wanted to practice in my future family, and to put to rest hurts that I had experienced, by fully accepting both the hurts and the joys, as they were. My twenties were also a time of growing closer to my parents and expressing gratitude for the incredible gifts they had instilled in me, as well as beginning to discuss as a family the generational wounds that in some form every family experiences.

I had prayed for years that God would bring me the right man at the right time. As a teen, I was very focused on my pro-life work, but I felt strongly that

God would bring my future husband—if I was meant to marry—in His timing. I also wanted my future marriage to be a mission marriage. I understood that marriage was a path to heaven, a path to learning to see Christ in one another and a path to growing closer to Him, but it was also a path to lead others to heaven. The world was on fire and needed help, needed work. What could I do? I wanted our marriage to be a part of the solution, as well as a partnership with my best friend. But, I also knew that marriage would never fulfill me in the way that only God can. The love I craved is ultimately found in the love of the Father and the gaze of Christ—no man could live up to Jesus, who was my first love. My mom even told me once, "You'll never marry if you expect him to be just like Jesus!" But I also knew that a future husband would, through his strengths and weaknesses, help me grow in my strengths and struggle against my weaknesses.

My single years before meeting Joe were not easy—in fact, they were very hard. The work for life—investigating the abortion industry, founding a national nonprofit and managing it, fund-raising and team building, international travel and speaking tours, media appearances, and the hostility I experienced, as well as the loneliness along the way—were all growing experiences. I learned that this life is not supposed to be easy—that doing hard things is *good*, when we are doing them for the right reasons. I learned that half the battle is not only our own striving, but our willingness to rest in the arms of our Father, both in our sleep at night and in adoration or sitting in silence with Him before the Blessed Sacrament. I learned that anything is possible with God, and that the teaching of the Church is a gift precious beyond compare, one we must delve more deeply into each day and treasure and guard. I also learned that we must be passionate —never to tire in struggling to love and serve souls (and fight for lives). I also learned important lessons about temptation: that in an angry and hurting world, it can be easy to get lost in our activism or even in identifying with political parties or groups—instead of keeping our identity first rooted

in Christ and making our relationship with Him our first priority.

These experiences and disciplines all prepared me for marriage. They also helped me to recognize the kind of man that I hoped for in a spouse. I dated a lot of good men and discovered more about myself and what I prized most in a future husband. I worked on becoming better myself, more self-aware, more virtuous, so I could be a good match for that future man. And as I continued growing in my Catholic faith and receiving formation, I came to understand that marriage is a path to heaven, a way of union with God, an opportunity to love Jesus intimately in your spouse and children.

When I met Joe, I knew quickly that he was someone I could marry. We shared similarities that surprised us: we are both from families of eight children, we were both raised in the Bay Area, and he is the oldest son and I the oldest daughter. We had both left the Bay Area for college and had come back after several years.

I had gone to Washington, DC, to open an office for Live Action, the pro-life organization I had founded in California. After attending the naval academy, Joe spent several years serving our country in the navy, traveling to Latin America, Asia, Europe, and the Middle East. I had also traveled internationally to Latin America, Europe, and other countries, speaking on the pro-life movement and my work investigating the abortion industry.

But back in the Bay Area I quickly realized, as did Joe, that God had brought us together and was giving us the invitation to love one another—and we could choose that freely. From the beginning, Joe was clear in his pursuit of me, but it took months of dating, and then engagement, to make clear his love and willingness to sacrifice for me. I was moved by Joe's desire to give his life for God and his future family, and I was impressed with all the hard work and planning he had put into that. I knew that this was a man who had the virtue and the desire to lead our family and who shared my vision for marriage. We also bonded over simpler things, such as our love for outdoor hikes and long conversations about history, theology, and public policy.

Looking back, getting married was one of the most natural things I've done in my life and was accompanied by many consolations. Now that we are married, Joe and I both experience the sacramental grace, a quiet but real presence, holding us up and providing protection for our love.

There are many things in American culture today that make it difficult for people to get married and even harder to stay married: our radical individualism; the severing of sex from commitment, intimacy and children; the high divorce rate; and a fundamental misunderstanding about what marriage means and the role of men and women. As Christians, we must avail ourselves of hearing and living the gospel—not just faithfully on Sundays, but every day, as best we can. We need Christ to sustain the love of a marriage. We need His reminders of sacrifice, His transformation

of the difficult and the painful into the redemptive, and His radical gift of forgiveness. We need the food of the Eucharist and frequent Confession.

Part of what Joe and I did to prepare for marriage as a couple was to meet with a mentor couple weekly. We read the Church's encyclicals on life, family, and marriage. We wrote each other letters sharing what we found challenging or inspiring and how the Church's teachings would inform our future marriage. We then read and discussed these letters with each other. We plan to continue the intentional work of studying our faith together and actively seeking to apply it to our relationship throughout our marriage.

As newlyweds, we know our work to grow in love has just begun. We know we can't do this without growing in our prayer life and personal formation— and persevering, despite busyness, difficulties, and distractions. I realize that how I love Joe is how I love Christ. My life with Joe is part of my life with Christ. How I treat Joe is how I treat Christ! When we are completely comfortable with and close to someone, we sometimes lose our refinement in how we love. Imagine going into Church and not genuflecting before entering the pew. These are little acts of love—yes, part of a routine, but designed for us to unite our hearts and bodies to what we know intellectually.

We are a work in progress, but we trust that God is the author of our marriage and that with Him, we can grow in love for each other. And we know that, if we let Him, God will use our marriage—including our mistakes and struggles as we grow—to show other people His love and bring them closer to Him.

Biographies

Katie Almon

Katie Almon is a fan of the saints in Heaven and on earth. She lives in New Orleans with her husband and two young children. Katie spent eight years working in Catholic education as both a high school teacher and campus minister. She now prays more than ever, begging for the grace to get through each day as a homeschooling mom. Katie has a master of arts in theological studies from Notre Dame Seminary in New Orleans.

Bobby Angel

Bobby Angel is a campus minister and theology teacher at an all-boys Catholic high school in California. He and his wife, Jackie, travel often to share the gospel and the call to a life of chastity. Bobby and Jackie also have recently begun a video ministry through Ascension Press's YouTube channel. They have three beautiful children who won't let them sleep. Connect with Bobby at jackieandbobby.com.

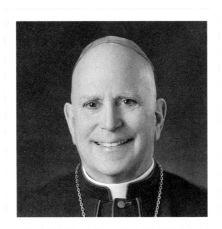

Archbishop Samuel J. Aquila

Samuel J. Aquila was ordained to the priesthood for the Archdiocese of Denver on June 5, 1976, and served in the archdiocese for twenty-five years. On March 18, 2002, he became bishop of Fargo, where he served until July 2012, when he was installed as the archbishop of Denver. Archbishop Aquila belongs to numerous boards and committees, including the Papal Foundation, the Bishops' Advisory Council for the Institute for Priestly Formation, and the Board of Trustees for the Augustine Institute. His episcopal motto comes from the Blessed Mother's instructions at Cana: "Do whatever he tells you" (John 2:5).

Sister John Thomas

Sister John Thomas Armour, O.P., grew up on a farm in Kansas as one of ten children. After graduating from the University of Dallas and serving on their study-abroad campus in Rome, she joined the Nashville-based Dominican Sisters of St. Cecilia in 2002. Serving at schools in Tennessee, South Carolina, Texas, and Minnesota, she has enjoyed teaching (and learning from) her students at the middle school and high school levels.

Jason Craig

Jason Craig writes from a small farm in western North Carolina. He is a convert to the Catholic Church and holds a master's degree in theology from the Augustine Institute. He is the cofounder of Fraternus, a fraternal organization that unites the men of a parish in brotherhood and provides the framework for them to mentor the next generation. Craig is also the editor of ThoseCatholicMen.com and founder of St. Joseph's Farm, where he hosts retreats that help men and their sons experience the joys and wisdom of traditional skills, crafts, and farming. Craig works alongside his wife, Katie, and their six children (five boys and one girl). He is also known to staunchly defend the claim that his family invented bourbon.

Sam Guzman

Sam Guzman is the founder and editor of The Catholic Gentleman (www.catholicgentleman.com) apostolate. He is the husband of Laura and father of four children. He lives in the rolling hills of the Oklahoma Ozarks, near Clear Creek Abbey, and works in marketing. Sam is an author, blogger, and occasional poet, and his work has appeared on *Catholic Exchange*, Aleteia, Truth and Charity Forum, and Jesus the Imagination as well as in the *Christian Science Monitor*. He is a frequent guest on various media programs.

Gemma Hawes

Gemma Hawes is a lover of all things creative. She is the graphic designer for *Valiant* and *Radiant* magazines, Catholic publications for young men and women. Although some days she wishes she were Joanna Gaines, Gemma is passionate about bringing a new face to Catholic print media. Born in South Africa and calling Atlanta, Georgia, home, her greatest joy in life is being a wife to Isaac and mother to her son, Logan.

Kelly J. Henson

Kelly J. Henson is a Catholic writer and speaker who explores the art of integrating faith into daily life. She lives in and explores with her husband and four children the beautiful North Carolina countryside. When she's not homeschooling, chasing unruly chickens, or scrubbing dishes, Kelly enjoys mountain hikes, reading, deep conversations over tea and homemade scones, and starting creative projects that she probably will not finish. Read more at kellyjhenson.com.

Brittany Makely

Brittany Makely, wife of her high school sweetheart and mother of four, lives in the heart of southern charm in North Carolina. She has worked as a researcher, writer, lobbyist, editor, and radio producer in the state-level public-policy arena and edited two national publications for young Catholic adults—*Radiant* for women and *Valiant* for men. Her greatest life's work, though, is attempting to make her family's house a home that embraces the fullness of the Catholic Faith, particularly through intentional liturgical living.

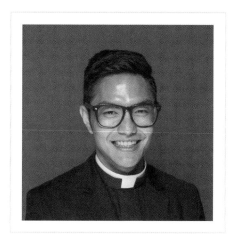

Deacon Raymond Philip Napuli

Raymond Philip Napuli is a transitional deacon for the Diocese of San Diego. He was born in the Philippines and grew up in Southern California. He has a profound appreciation for music and love for the Faith. While he was studying at the Conservatory of Music at the University of the Pacific, a chance visit to a Carmelite monastery led him to discern a priestly vocation, which he pursued shortly after graduation. Deacon Raymond Philip is currently finishing his formation at Mount Angel Seminary in St. Benedict, Oregon, and hopes to be ordained a priest in 2020.

Rose Rea

Rose Rea is the founder of *Valiant* and *Radiant*, Catholic publications for young men and women. A native of a small town in North Dakota and a country girl at heart, she treasures the gift of our Catholic Faith, passed down by her parents, especially the rich writings of the Doctors of the Church. Saying yes to God's will and being a wife and mother of five children is her greatest joy.

Lila Rose

Lila Rose is a speaker, writer, and human-rights activist. Lila founded and serves as president of Live Action, a media and news nonprofit dedicated to ending abortion and inspiring a culture that respects all human life. Live Action's groundbreaking news coverage and compelling videos reach several million people weekly across Facebook, Twitter, YouTube, and Instagram.

Matthew Samson

Matthew Samson is a seminarian studying for the Diocese of Fargo. He was born and raised in North Dakota and enjoys hunting and fishing. After pursuing a career in business, he felt called by the Blessed Mother to pursue a vocation to the priesthood. He is currently a first-year pre-theology student at Mount Saint Mary's Seminary in Emmitsburg, Maryland. He would like to thank all of the faithful for their prayers for religious vocations.

Dr. Andrew Swafford

Andrew Swafford is associate professor of theology at Benedictine College. He is a general editor and contributor to *The Great Adventure Catholic Bible*, published by Ascension Press, and the author of *Nature and Grace, John Paul II to Aristotle and Back Again*, and *Spiritual Survival in the Modern World.* He holds a doctorate in sacred theology from the University of St. Mary of the Lake and a master's degree in Old Testament and Semitic languages from Trinity Evangelical Divinity School. He lives with his wife, Sarah, and their five children in Atchison, Kansas.

Kendra Tierney

Kendra Tierney is a wife and mother of nine children from newborn to teenager. She's a homeschooler and a regular schooler, and an enthusiastic amateur experimenter in the domestic arts. She writes the award-winning Catholic mommy blog *Catholic All Year*, is a regular contributor to Blessed Is She Ministries, and is the voice of liturgical living at Endow Ministries. She is the author of *A Little Book about Confession for Children* and *The Catholic All Year Compendium: Liturgical Living for Real Life.*

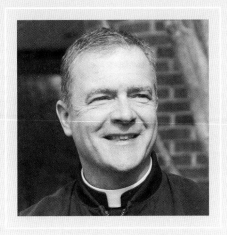

Father Phil Tighe

Father Phil Tighe grew up in the Sandhills of North Carolina and is a graduate of The Citadel, Kenan-Flagler Business School, and Catholic University. He entered priestly formation for the Diocese of Raleigh at age thirty-two. He was commissioned in the US Navy to serve as a navy chaplain and was ordained a priest at Sacred Heart Parish in Pinehurst in 2000. He is currently serving as the pastor of St. Thomas Aquinas Parish. He also serves as the director of vocations and the director of Seminarian Formation for the Diocese of Raleigh. He firmly believes that every person has a vocation, a calling from God. Finding it is the fruit of prayer and when it's found, what great joy!

Peter Weldon

Peter Weldon lives in the Chicago suburbs with his wife of thirty-four years. They are the blessed parents of two children and a growing family of beautiful grandchildren. After more than thirty years in the tech industry, Peter now devotes his energies to the local food pantry and to pursuing his lifelong passion for photography. He is honored to have his work featured in *Spirit and Life* alongside such powerful and vulnerable testaments about the sacraments.

Image Credits

All photography featured is by Peter Weldon unless specified below.

We want to share our extreme gratitude with the Catholic churches who let us capture the beauty within their sacred spaces for this book. With special thanks to:

Holy Family Catholic Community
2515 West Palatine Road, Inverness, IL 60067
Featured on page 129

St. Catherine of Siena Catholic Church
845 West Main Street, West Dundee, IL 60118
Featured on pages 31, 62, 157

St. Catherine of Siena Chapel (Chapel on the Rock)
Camp St. Malo, 10758 State Highway 7, Allenspark, CO 80510
Featured on pages 88, 89, 105

St. Clement Catholic Church
642 West Deming Place, Chicago, IL 60614
Featured on pages 27, 38, 41, 45, 49, 65, 75, 118, 121

St. Finbarr's Oratory
Gougane Barra, County Cork, Ireland
Featured on pages 12, 13

St. Ita Catholic Church
1220 West Catalpa Avenue, Chicago, IL 60640
Featured on pages XII, 18, 68, 125, 148

St. Joan of Arc Catholic Church
820 Division Street, Lisle, IL 60532
Featured on page 55

St. John Cantius Catholic Church
825 North Carpenter Street, Chicago, IL 60642
Featured on the cover and on pages 51, 81, 85, 97, 123

St. Michael Catholic Church
1633 North Cleveland Avenue, Chicago, IL 60614
Featured on pages II, XIV, 7, 59, 73, 94, 183, 187

Memorial Statue to Infants and Unborn by Knights of Columbus Council 654, Elgin, IL
Featured on page 33

Quin Abbey
Quin, County Clare, Ireland
Featured on pages 142-143

Cliffs of Moher, County Clare, Ireland
Featured on the Masthead

Anderson Japanese Gardens, Rockford, IL
Featured on page 21

Barrington Hills, IL
Featured on page 99

Photo by Natasha Rider
Featured on page 112

Matthiessen State Park, IL
Featured on page 137

Photo by Andrew Wright/*Denver Catholic*,
courtesy of the Diocese of Denver
Featured on page 151

Photo Courtesy of Diocese of Raleigh
Featured on page 161

Photo by Anne Puezter
Featured on page 164, 206

Photos by Sharayah and Bence Fonyad
Featured on pages 170, 173

Photo by Raluca Rodila
Featured on page 177

Photo by Heidi Ryder
Featured on page 191

Photo by Julie Samson
Featured on page 208

"For where your treasure is, there also will your heart be" (Matt. 6:21). This book is dedicated to my Creator for my most prized treasure, my eternal soul. My heart belongs to Him, who has given everything to offer us eternal life. May each person realize the precious gift that is his or her own soul, especially my five little children, whose souls I have been entrusted with—oh, what love I have for you and your father! Finally, to my beautiful Blessed Mother, what an honor to be named after the roses at your feet. Mary, Mother of Love, pray for us.

—**Rose**

I dedicate this book to all priests, religious, and married couples. My prayer is that this book opens our hearts and minds and makes us fall more deeply in love with our Faith and with Jesus Christ by learning the truth about each blessed sacrament. I want this book, by teaching the basics and blessings of each sacrament, to assist the lost souls in the Church who are struggling.

—**Gemma**

Sophia Institute

Sophia Institute is a nonprofit institution that seeks to nurture the spiritual, moral, and cultural life of souls and to spread the Gospel of Christ in conformity with the authentic teachings of the Roman Catholic Church.

Sophia Institute Press fulfills this mission by offering translations, reprints, and new publications that afford readers a rich source of the enduring wisdom of mankind. Sophia Institute also operates two popular online Catholic resources: CrisisMagazine.com and CatholicExchange.com.

Crisis Magazine provides insightful cultural analysis that arms readers with the arguments necessary for navigating the ideological and theological minefields of the day. Catholic Exchange provides world news from a Catholic perspective as well as daily devotionals and articles that will help you to grow in holiness and live a life consistent with the teachings of the Church.

In 2013, Sophia Institute launched Sophia Institute for Teachers to renew and rebuild Catholic culture through service to Catholic education. With the goal of nurturing the spiritual, moral, and cultural life of souls, and an abiding respect for the role and work of teachers, we strive to provide materials and programs that are at once enlightening to the mind and ennobling to the heart; faithful and complete, as well as useful and practical.

Sophia Institute gratefully recognizes the Solidarity Association for preserving and encouraging the growth of our apostolate over the course of many years. Without their generous and timely support, this book would not be in your hands.

www.SophiaInstitute.com
www.CatholicExchange.com
www.CrisisMagazine.com
www.SophiaInstituteforTeachers.org

Sophia Institute Press® is a registered trademark of Sophia Institute.
Sophia Institute is a tax-exempt institution as defined by the
Internal Revenue Code, Section 501(c)(3). Tax I.D. 22-2548708.